Problem Regions of Europe

General Editor **D. I. Scargill**

The Paris Basin
Ian B. Thompson

OXFORD UNIVERSITY PRESS 1973

Oxford University Press, Ely House, London W. 1

GLASGOW NEW YORK TORONTO MELBOURNE WELLINGTON
CAPE TOWN IBADAN NAIROBI DAR ES SALAAM LUSAKA ADDIS ABABA
DELHI BOMBAY CALCUTTA MADRAS KARACHI LAHORE DACCA
KUALA LUMPUR SINGAPORE HONG KONG TOKYO

Photoset by BAS Printers Limited, Wallop, Hampshire
and printed in Great Britain at the University Press, Oxford,
by Vivian Ridler, Printer to the University

Editor's Preface

Great economic and social changes have taken place in Europe in recent years. The agricultural labour force has almost everywhere contracted, in some places very rapidly, and the lack of alternative forms of employment in rural areas has resulted in large-scale movements of farmers and farm labourers in search of work in the cities. The scale of this drift from the land can be gauged from the fact that in the six (original) Common Market countries the agricultural work force was halved between 1950 and 1970: from approximately 20 millions to 10 millions. In many areas this rural exodus has made it possible to carry out much needed reorganization of farm holdings, but it has also brought with it problems concerning, for example, the provision of services to a contracting population and the need to establish new forms of land use where farming is no longer profitable.

Contraction of the labour force has also taken place in several old-established industries. These include coal-mining, shipbuilding, and the more traditional textile industries, where the effects of a shrinking market have been made more severe by automation, which has substituted machines for men. The coal-mining industry of Western Europe shed something like two-thirds of its labour force during the 1950s and 1960s. Wherever a large proportion of the working population was dependent upon a declining industry of this kind, the problems of adjustment have been severe. Many schemes have been devised to attract alternative forms of employment but, despite incentives, it has often proved difficult to attract new firms because of the old industrial areas' legacy of dirt, derelict landscape, poor housing, and, in some places, bad labour relations.

Problems of a different kind have arisen as a result of the continued growth of large cities such as London and Paris, or of groups of closely related cities as in the case of Randstad Holland. The reasons for such growth are several. To the manufacturer the big city offers the advantage of a local market, a varied labour force, and easy access to suppliers and other manufacturers with whom he needs to maintain close links. To them and even more to the service industries a city location offers a prestige location, and the enormous expansion of service activity, especially office-work, has contributed greatly to postwar urban growth. Attempts to control the increase of employment within cities have had some success as far as manufacturing industry is concerned but very little with regard to office work.

Problems resulting from city growth include traffic congestion, high land prices, pollution, and social stress brought about by factors such as housing shortages and travelling long distances to work. Yet the city continues to attract migrants for whom the image is still one of streets paved with gold, whilst the established resident is loath to leave the 'bright lights', the football club, or the familiar shops.

Geographers, in the past, have been reluctant to focus their attention on regional problems. The problem was thought to be a temporary phenomenon and therefore less worthy of consideration than regional characteristics of a more enduring nature—the landscape or the chimerical *personality* of the region. Yet such is the magnitude, persistence, and areal extent of problems of the kind referred to above that the geographer would seem to be well justified in approaching his regional study by seeking to identify, measure, and even seek solutions to problems. 'Devenant alors un cadre de recherche, la région sera choisie en fonction de certains problèmes et des moyens qui permettent de les aborder avec profit' (H. Baulig). Indeed it has been suggested that regions can be defined in terms of the problems with which they are confronted.

Additional stimulus for studying regional problems arises from the interest which politicians and planners have recently shown in the region as a framework for tackling such issues as the relief of unemployment, the siting of new investment, and the reorganization of administrative boundaries. Governments have long been aware of the problems resulting from economic and social changes and various attempts have been made to solve them. Development Areas and New Towns in Great Britain, for example, represent an attempt to deal with the problems, on the one hand, of the declining industrial areas and, on the other, of the overgrown cities. Such solutions can hardly be described as regional, however. Other countries have recognized the problems of their overpopulated rural areas and the Cassa per il

Mezzogiorno, the Fund for the South, was set up by the Italian government in 1950 in order to encourage investment in the South. The E.E.C. has also channelled funds via its Investment Bank, both to southern Italy and to other parts of the Common Market distant from the main centres of economic activity. Planning of this kind shows an awareness of the regional extent of economic and social problems, though in practice much of the actual work of planning was undertaken on a piecemeal, local, and short-term basis.

Since about 1960, however, the continuing nature of the problems has persuaded most European governments to adopt longer-term and more comprehensive planning measures, and the importance of seeking regional solutions has been increasingly stressed. The last ten years have, in fact, witnessed the setting up of regional planning authorities in many European countries and to them has been given the task of identifying regional problems and of finding solutions to them. A large number of reports have been published following research carried out by these authorities, and individual governments have introduced regional considerations to national planning. The French *métropoles d'équilibre,* for example, were devised in order to introduce new vigour to the regions via the largest provincial towns.

One of the drawbacks to regional planning of this kind is the outdated nature of local government boundaries, most planning decisions having to be implemented through a system of local government more suited to nineteenth than to late twentieth century conditions. Some experts have thus advocated a regional alternative to existing local government areas, and it is interesting to note that the Royal Commission on Local Government in England (the Maud Report), whilst not supporting so radical a change, nevertheless introduced the idea of *provinces* within which broad planning policies could be carried out. Supporters of the regional idea argue that a growing trend toward State centralization is bringing about a reaction in the form of renewed popular interest in regions, their history, industrial archaeology, customs, dialect, and so on.

The revival of interest in regions, both for their own sake and as a practical aid to planning or administration, makes particularly timely the appearance of a series of geographical studies concerned with *Problem Regions of Europe*. The present volume is one of 12 studies comprising such a series.

The twelve regions have been selected in order to illustrate, between them, a variety of problems. The most obvious of these are: problems of a harsh environment, of isolation, of industrial decay, of urban congestion, and of proximity to a sensitive political frontier. One or other of these major problems forms the dominant theme in each of the volumes of the series, but they have not been studied in isolation. Where it has been thought relevant to do so, authors have drawn attention to similar problems encountered in other parts of the continent so that readers may compare both the causes of problems and the methods employed to solve them. At the same time it is recognized that every region has a number of problems that are unique to itself and these peculiarly local problems have been distinguished from those of a more general kind.

Although the precise treatment of each subject will vary according to the nature of the region concerned and, to some extent, the outlook of a particular author, readers will find much in common in the arrangement of contents in each volume. In each of them the nature of the problem or problems which characterize the region is first stated by the author; next the circumstances that have given rise to the problems are explained; after this the methods that have been employed to overcome the problems are subjected to critical examination and evaluation. Each study includes indications of likely future developments.

All the authors of the series have considerable first-hand knowledge of the regions about which they have written. Yet none of them would claim to have a complete set of answers to any particular regional problem. For this reason, as well as from a desire to make the series challenging, each volume contains suggestions for further lines of inquiry that the reader may pursue. The series was conceived initially as one that would be helpful to sixth-form geographers but it is believed that individual volumes will also provide a useful introduction to the detailed work undertaken by more advanced students both of geography and of European studies in general.

D.I.S.

St. Edmund Hall,
August 1972

Contents

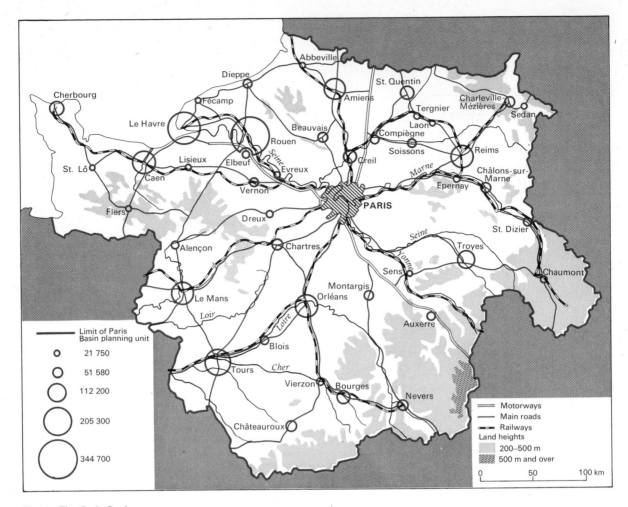

Fig. 1. The Paris Basin

Introduction

The Paris Basin is probably the region of France most intensively studied in British schools and universities. This reflects its proximity to Britain, its crucial importance to the French economy, and also its role in the inspiration of classical French regional geography. The rhythmic alternation of scarp and vale and the close association of rock type and cultural landscape has imprinted on the Paris Basin a mosaic of *pays*, small-scale regions, each with an individual geographical personality. The rapid economic changes during recent decades have served to blur this landscape differentiation, but the *pays* are still commonly employed as conventional units in school texts as a means of studying the geography of the Paris Basin.

This book seeks to portray the region in a different and dual perspective. Rather than viewing the Paris Basin as an aggregate of *pays*, the unity is seen in the polarizing effects of the Paris agglomeration. Paris exerts powerful attractive effects on both population and resources throughout the Basin, and at the same time emits vital economic, cultural, and political currents. Secondly, unlike most texts, which stress the wealth and success of the region, this book presents it as a problem area and a potential victim of its economic success unless far-sighted planning is undertaken. Viewed in these perspectives, it is not considered necessary to describe in detail the elements of physical geography abundantly covered in existing books. Instead, emphasis is placed on the Paris Basin as a functional unit, based on a specific organization of population, resources, and space, as a framework for discussion of the many problems which exist in this context.

The geographical context

At first sight, the Paris Basin might seem an unlikely choice as a problem region. The vast expanses of fertile agricultural land, the expanding and prosperous regional centres, and the obvious vitality of the Paris agglomeration indicate a region enjoying outstanding success rather than difficulty. In fact, it is this economic success which makes the Paris Basin an excellent example of a problem region of a relatively new kind—the city region polarized by a major world city, the rapid growth of which imposes enormous problems of social and economic organization. The problems of the Paris Basin thus stem directly from the exceptional character of the great city at its heart. Paris is exceptional in the extent to which it occupies a dominant position in each of its three main geographical contexts; as a world city, as primate city of France, and as the metropolitan centre of the Paris Basin.

Paris is the third largest city in the world, with 8·2 million inhabitants in its agglomeration in 1968. Its eminence as a world city does not, however, rest primarily on its vast population—for this is a relatively modern feature—but rather on a complex web of international relations built up over centuries. Paris fulfils a world role in the spheres of trade, finance, transport, cultural, and political organization, inherited from a colonial past and perpetuated by the present status of France as an expanding industrial nation and an influential political force. This international importance finds its counterpart within the nation, for Paris is in every sense the primate city of France. The Paris agglomeration is eight times more populous than its nearest rivals, Lyon and Marseille, and its position at the head of the hierarchy of French cities is unchallenged. In terms of the concentration of economic and political power, affluence, and cultural activity, Paris enjoys a superiority in France widely held to be excessive. The strength of Paris is even more emphatic in its function as the metropolitan centre of the Paris Basin. The growth of provincial centres within the Basin has been stifled by the development of Paris, and the largest regional centres: Rouen (370 000 inhabitants), Le Havre (250 000), Tours (200 000), Reims, Orléans, and Le Mans (170 000), are essentially subordinate to Paris (Fig. 1).

Each of these three geographical contexts, world, primate, and metropolitan city, has created strong forces of economic growth which have sustained demographic expansion, which in turn reinforced the predominance of Paris. The position has now been reached where the fulfilment of these three roles has created problems, the effects of which are not confined to the agglomeration but which reach out into the Paris Basin.

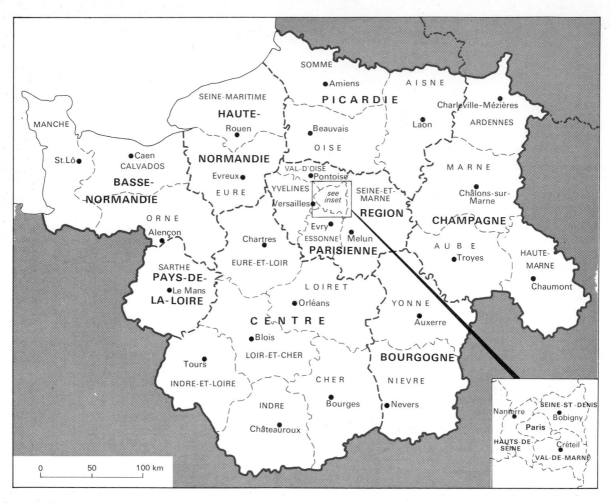

Fig. 2. The Paris Basin planning unit

The problem of definition

The term 'Paris Basin' is of geological rather than geographical origin and the definition of its extent corresponds with the distribution of Secondary and Tertiary rocks deposited in the vast sedimentary basin of northern and north-eastern France. The structural boundary is very clearly defined where the sedimentary rocks come into contact with the adjacent Hercynian massifs of Armorica, the Massif Central, the Vosges, and the Ardennes. Between these massifs the boundary is less clear in Artois, southern Lorraine, and Poitou, where minor relief features rather than rock type mark the limits of the Basin. By this structural definition, the Paris Basin covers an area of 140 000 square kilometres, or over one-quarter of the national land area. Geological criteria do not, however, provide a satisfactory definition in relation to development problems. In particular, Lorraine must be considered as being

separate in identity from the remainder of the structural basin: the discordant drainage runs northwards, away from the Seine system; the plateaux are more elevated and lower in agricultural value; above all, the deposits of coal, iron and salt have inspired a pattern of industrial and urban development totally different from that of the remainder of the Basin.

In the context of the Paris Basin as a problem region it is essential to define the area in terms that correspond with the distribution of problems affecting Paris and its city region, rather than impose arbitrary geological limits. Such a definition is provided by the official government planning unit of the Paris Basin, designated as a framework for long-term planning and currently employed in the execution of the Sixth National Plan (1971–5). This unit (Fig. 2) excludes Lorraine and much smaller portions of the structural basin in Poitou and Artois. It does, however, include the whole

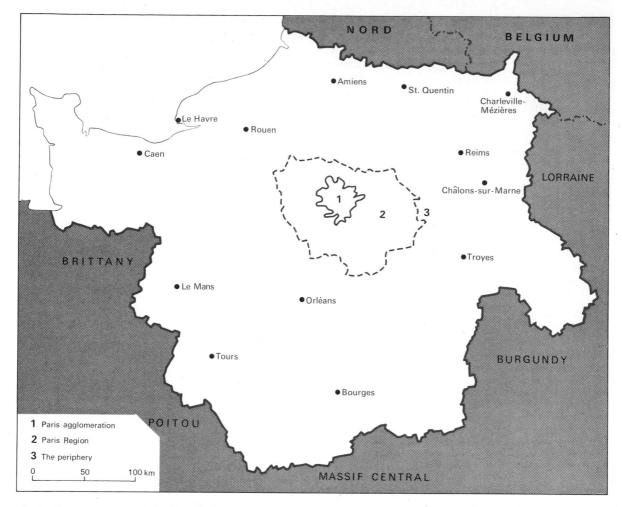

Fig. 3. The components of the Paris Basin

of the Paris Basin directly influenced by Paris and within which an effort of co-ordinated regional planning is being made. The term 'Paris Basin' will be applied consistently with this connotation throughout the text.

The components of the Paris Basin

Within the overall symmetry of scarpland topography the Paris Basin includes a great variety of physical environments. In terms of planning problems this diversity can be generalized into three areal components: the Paris agglomeration, the Paris Region, and the peripheral zone (Fig. 3).

The Paris agglomeration has a star-shaped morphology resulting from generations of suburban expansion along routeways radiating from the city. A distinction can thus be drawn between the city proper, approximately coterminous with the *département* of Paris, and the inner and outer suburban rings which spread out into the adjacent

départements of Hauts-de-Seine, Seine-St.-Denis, and Val-de-Marne. The agglomeration is the focal point of the Paris Region, the administrative and planning unit currently being employed as a framework for the future expansion of Paris. The Paris Region corresponds approximately with the central core of the geological basin, consisting of ·Tertiary limestones, sands, and sandstones, dissected by the Seine and its major tributaries the Oise and Marne. The valleys are the main transport arteries, the rivers being canalized and the valley floors followed by main road and rail. The valleys are thus the site of urbanization while the plateaux are occupied by arable farming and by extensive forests. The influence of Paris is supreme throughout the region and its prime function is to serve the needs of Paris in terms of agricultural produce, transport arteries, recreational zones, and also as a residential zone for a commuting population.

The remainder of the Paris Basin, by far the largest proportion in area, may be termed peripheral, as opposed to the core area already indicated. It consists predominantly of rolling chalk plains, but in the east the alternation of scarp and vale is more pronounced. In the Cotentin peninsula, and to a lesser extent in the Ardennes, portions of the crystalline fringe of the geological basin are included. The agricultural landscape is characterized by a dominance of arable over pastoral land-uses, except in the *bocage* of Lower Normandy where high grade dairy farming is well developed, in Champagne Humide, where pasture again prevails, and in the well-wooded Ardennes. In general, the peripheral zone is characterized by advanced farming techniques, relatively large farms, a high proportion of tenancy, and, by French standards, well consolidated farm holdings. The large expanses of fertile limon soils and the use of artificial fertilizers make this the most productive agricultural zone of France. The main urban centres of the periphery are distributed in an aureola circling Paris, often referred to as the *couronne*, at a distance of from 120 to 200 kilometres. These towns are regional centres and transport foci which until recently relied on such traditional industries based on the produce of their hinterlands as food processing, textiles, wood-, leather- and glass-working, together with light engineering firms. Exceptionally, by virtue of their port function, Le Havre and Rouen developed heavier branches of industry, including heavy engineering and chemicals. Essentially these towns developed as centres for predominantly rural hinterlands, acting as collecting and distribution centres and supplying administrative and commercial services. Their expansion was, however, stifled by the proximity of Paris and until recently the regional centres were characterized by their slow growth and narrow economic base, and their prime function was as staging posts for both goods and people destined for Paris. Since 1945 the towns of the *couronne* have undergone a rapid change; new industry, much of it decentralized from Paris, has stimulated economic growth and their population has risen rapidly. Their new dynamism makes them key points in the future planning of the Paris Basin. Nevertheless, their size is still insignificant as compared with that of the metropolis; with the exception of Rouen and Le Havre, all have under 200 000 inhabitants. The location of the regional centres, on routes radiating from Paris, gives the Paris Basin as a whole quite a regular pattern of urbanization. In a limited number of cases, the existence of the routeway has stimulated a marked linear pattern of urbanization. This applies particularly in the lower Seine valley where industrial and port expansion is producing a rapid urbanization of the corridor linking Paris to its maritime outlets at Rouen and Le Havre. On a smaller scale, the Oise valley and the middle Loire valley are experiencing similar linear patterns of urban growth.

The problems which must now be discussed thus have as their background a massive agglomeration of exceptional size and strength, set in a core region entirely dominated by Paris, and surrounded by an extensive peripheral zone, formerly tributary to Paris but now caught up in the growth process.

1 The Problems of the Paris Basin

The everyday problems of Paris are essentially those confronting any large European city. The congestion of traffic, the demand for more and better housing, the need to renew large urban tracts, the modernization of services and administration, are all problems common to the great conurbations and metropolises of Europe. If the problems of Paris are commonplace, they are nevertheless increased in severity by three main considerations. The high degree of primacy enjoyed by Paris imposes certain strains on the city while at the same time depriving the provincial regions of potential growth. Secondly, the scale of the agglomeration is such that the normal problems of transport congestion, urban renewal, and the accommodation of new growth, are invested with a magnitude shared only by a limited number of cities in Europe. Thirdly, as a consequence of the size and strength of Paris, the problems of the agglomeration are not confined to the built-up area, but are projected outwards into the Paris Basin. This summary of problems is thus cast in the triple perspective of the nation, the agglomeration, and the Paris Basin region.

Paris and the nation

Paris in relation to France has been likened to a head that has grown too large for its body. This excessive weight results from the demographic and economic expansion of Paris in modern times, and also from the extreme concentration of the power of decision vested in the Capital.

The demographic supremacy of Paris is apparent from the fact that although occupying only 2·2 per cent of the national land area, the Paris Region accounted for 18 per cent of the total population of France in 1968, and almost 30 per cent of the urban population. In crude terms therefore, approximately every fifth Frenchman and almost one in every three urban dwellers lives in the Paris Region. This degree of concentration is a modern feature. A century ago only 8 per cent of the national population lived in the Paris Region and at the end of the nineteenth century the proportion had risen to only 11 per cent. Between 1901 and 1945 the total population of France actually declined marginally but that of the Paris Region increased by over 40 per cent, and its share of the national total rose to 16 per cent. It is only in the last decade that the growth of Paris has been matched by that of the nation as a whole.

Underlying the modern surge of population growth has been rapid economic development, for it has been the opportunity to obtain remunerative employment which has attracted the large number of migrants making up a significant proportion of the total increase. A chain reaction has been established whereby the attraction of population to available employment has enlarged the regional market, in turn creating more employment and additional migration. In this process, linkages have been established between related and inter-dependent industries; head offices and research facilities became established in Paris, and the massive apparatus of supporting activities in commerce, banking, transport, and administration crystallized. Thus, the advanced technological industries, on which the post-war revival of the French economy has been based, initially found optimum locations in the Paris Region with its large market, skilled labour pools, commercial institutions, and highly developed transport systems. This conferred on Paris the advantage of having advanced industries involving a high added-value to raw materials and semi-finished components, experiencing high growth rates, and able to support wage levels above the national average in industry generally.

The quasi-monopoly of the power of decision vested in Paris stems from the extreme centralization of government administration and also from the universal tendency for firms to locate their head offices in the city, even when their productive capacity is located elsewhere in France. The centralization of government has led to absurd extremes of administrative complexity, a proliferation of the civil service sector and a general remoteness of the point of decision from the areas and population directly affected by the decisions. As in the case of industrial employment, the effect of centralization has been to provide Paris with a range of opportunities and higher wage levels in the tertiary sector than those obtaining in the Provinces.

The net result of the concentration of population, economic activity, and direction of the nation's affairs in a single small region has been to endow Paris with an excessive degree of opportunity, wealth, and power to the detriment of the Provinces. In particular, the primacy of Paris has to some extent stifled the growth of French regional capitals and inhibited their capacity to stimulate and direct the economic expansion of their tributary regions. The opposition between Paris and the Provinces has been the subject of much debate since 1945, and the phrase 'Paris and the French Desert', referring to the contrast between an allegedly parasitic capital and the economic and cultural wilderness of the Provinces, has entered into everyday language. It is therefore important to establish the true scale of the disparity, since the situation is open to exces-

sive dramatization. The situation is best reviewed in the mid 1960s, since when major efforts of decentralization have been introduced, these being evaluated at a later stage in the text.

Paris and the French desert
With over four million workers in 1968, the Paris Region employed 21 per cent of the total French labour force. This proportion increases substantially in the case of more qualified employment. Thus 39 per cent of the professional and managerial grades, 48 per cent of the qualified engineers, and 72 per cent of the nation's research

Fig. 4. The Paris agglomeration

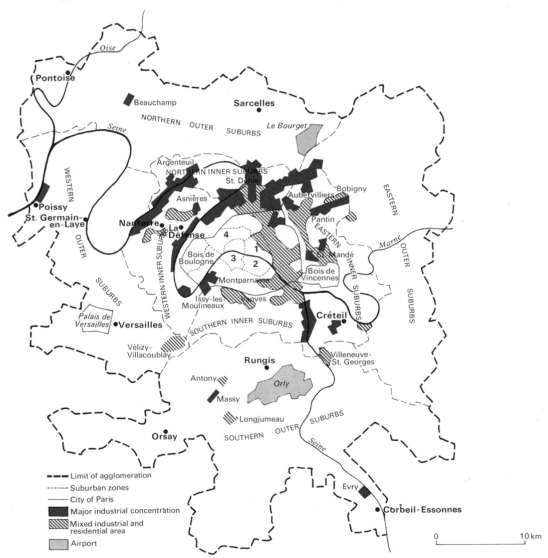

TABLE 1
The population of the Paris agglomeration

	Population 1968	Change 1962–8 per cent	Change due to migration per cent
Paris City	2 581 796	−7·0	−10·2
Inner suburban ring			
north	557 913	9·8	3·3
east	756 226	6·6	1·7
south	826 748	8·5	4·1
west	870 232	5·0	−1·5
Outer suburban ring			
north	530 777	33·6	26·1
east	610 900	27·2	20·4
south	864 127	37·7	30·2
west	583 522	21·7	15·3
Total agglomeration	8 182 241	7·9	2·9

workers were employed in the Paris Region in 1968. At this time, Paris accounted for 56 per cent by value of the output of the aircraft industry, 80 per cent of car production, 68 per cent of precision engineered products, and 75 per cent of the national output of radio and television sets. In total, the region contributed 35 per cent by value of the nation's exports.

The Capital monopolizes the head offices of banking and insurance and 64 per cent of all French registered companies were directed from Paris in 1968. The nation's cultural life is equally concentrated, the city having a virtual monopoly of radio and television, the most prestigious university and professional institutions, and a pre-eminence in all aspects of artistic expression. In purely material terms the average income in the Paris Region, as measured by the earnings of the head of household, was double that of the under-developed regions of western France, and between 20 and 30 per cent higher than that of the more advanced regions of eastern France. Given that opportunities for female employment are greater and better remunerated in Paris than elsewhere, the true disparity in income levels is even wider.

The apparent social and material advantages of Paris over the Provinces are to some extent depreciated by the fact that Paris has a much higher cost of living and suffers more acute housing shortages, serious traffic congestion, tiring and expensive journey to work movements and atmospheric pollution. Nevertheless, the fact remains that in terms of economic strength, cultural provision, and the power to direct the national life, Paris enjoys a degree of concentration that is widely held to be excessive. It does not follow that had the growth of Paris been restrained, the surplus growth would have been more evenly distributed elsewhere. Much of the success of Paris derives from its location within France and in relation to Western Europe, and it is the exploitation of this advantage which has created growth. It has, nevertheless, been official policy during the last decade to attempt to redress the imbalance between Paris and the Provinces. In particular an effort is being made to counterbalance Paris with effective regional capitals, which must function not only as economic growth poles but also as genuine centres of direction in industry, business, culture, and administration. This policy has thus been marked by attempts to divert activity from Paris to benefit the regional capitals and at the same time alleviate some of the less-appreciated consequences of rapid growth which are now assuming serious proportions within the agglomeration.

Problems of the Paris agglomeration
The type and severity of problems within the agglomeration vary according to the functional zones. In particular, the distinction between the city proper and the inner and outer suburban rings is of great importance (Fig. 4).

Table 1 indicates that the recent growth of Paris has been achieved overwhelmingly by the

Photo 1. View north-east across the commercial and business quarter of central Paris. In the foreground is the Grand Palais and (right) Place de la Concorde. In the distance, beyond the Butte Montmartre with the Church of Sacré Coeur are the industrial suburbs of St. Denis and Aubervilliers

process of suburban extension. The city of Paris declined by 7 per cent between 1962 and 1968, due to a migratory loss of almost 300 000 inhabitants. The inner suburbs expanded at a rate close to that of the agglomeration as a whole, and it was in the outer suburbs that the most dramatic gains were recorded. In the agglomeration as a whole, migration from other regions of France accounted for only one-third of the total population increase and it follows that the main changes in population distribution are being brought about by natural increase and by movement of population from the centre towards the periphery of the agglomeration.

The city of Paris

The city has a roughly circular form, with two-thirds of it located on the right bank of the Seine. Its structure consists of a core area, subdivided into specialized functional zones, surrounded by predominantly residential areas with varying degrees of industrial activity.

The heart of the city is the historic core, situated on the right bank to the north of the Ile de la Cité (zone 1 in Fig. 4). It contains many of the city's finest buildings and monuments set in a dense mosaic of commercial and residential building dating from the eighteenth and nineteenth centuries. With the exception of a few fine boulevards the built-up area is punctuated by narrow streets and apart from the Tuileries gardens there are few large open spaces. Towards its eastern fringe there is a marked concentration of small-scale and artisan industries and a deterioration in the age and quality of housing. The main railway termini are located at the outer limit of this historic and commercial core.

The dominant problem of this zone is that of congestion. As the major concentration of office, retail, and service activities in Paris the daily influx of commuters is enormous, while the general level of circulation induced by its commercial activity ensures continuous dense traffic throughout the daytime. The problems of traffic density are compounded by the narrowness of most streets, the limited street-parking capacity, and the convergence of traffic on certain strategic intersections, the railway termini, and the Seine bridges. A second problem is that of the renewal of large areas of older buildings, particularly in the east, characterized by their dilapidated condition and anarchic inter-mixture of residential, commercial and semi-industrial usage. The decision to close the Halles food market is symptomatic of the problems both of traffic congestion and the need for physical renovation. A general tendency has been manifest for many years for business activity to gravitate westwards away from the old core of the city.

The central zone of the city is counterbalanced on the left bank by the intellectual and university quarter of Paris, centred on the twin axes of the Boulevard St. Michel and the Boulevard St. Germain. The problem of congestion is only relatively less severe than on the right bank for the cultural function is serviced by a high density of bookshops, publishing houses, cinemas, restaurants, hotels, and administrative buildings. The combination of university institutions of world renown and a vast tourist influx make this the most cosmopolitan quarter of Paris. There is much older housing in the east of this zone, and on the southern fringe the rebuilt Montparnasse railway terminus is the scene of a major renewal scheme involving office development.

To the west of this Latin Quarter is a remarkable concentration of government administrative buildings, spilling over onto the right bank (zone 3 in Fig. 4). Here, close to the Chamber of Deputies, are to be found the main ministerial departments, together with many commercial and professional administrative offices. The residential density is low, and apart from the inevitable problems of circulation this is a stable portion of the city relatively free from severe planning problems.

The core of the city is completed on the right bank by a linear zone extending from the Place de la Concorde and the Opéra to the Étoile (zone 4) which is essentially a continuation of the central business district. It may be distinguished by the concentration of head offices of major national and international firms, newspaper and publicity houses, luxury hotels and shops. In comparison with the central commercial zone, this area has an atmosphere of luxury and prestige, has more modern buildings, and is manifestly a major centre of power and influence in the nation's industrial and commercial life. As compared with the erosion of commercial activity in the historic core, this area is gradually extending westwards into the inner suburb of Neuilly. The four broad zones of the city core are surrounded by predominantly residential areas of varying style and quality. In general the quality of the urban environment is higher in the west than in the east, where industrial activity is more generally intermingled with residential land use.

The planning problems of the city are thus essentially those resulting from the congestion of traffic and buildings, in turn the product of the concentration of activity into a relatively small area. It follows that to relieve this congestion implies the halting and even reversal of growth processes established over centuries and consolidated during the last hundred years. Traffic congestion may be relieved by the improved integration, speed, and capacity of the transport systems. The physical congestion of the built-up area may be alleviated by comprehensive renewal involving the creation of open spaces. Both these processes may be facilitated by the decentralization of activities from central Paris. However, the constraints on such developments are severe for they must be executed without compromising the unique aspects of the city, especially its heritage of historical buildings. They must also be enacted against a background of the highest land values in France, which imposes serious financial constraints.

The inner suburban ring

The inner ring of suburbs is constituted by a zone contiguous to the city and almost entirely built up, which expanded during the nineteenth century absorbing the pre-existing settlement. The most obvious contrast with the city lies in the high level of industrialization, for the agglomeration's major industrial concentrations are located here, along the banks of the Seine and near the canals and railways radiating from central Paris.

The northern inner suburbs extend from Argenteuil in the west to Aubervilliers in the east and shelter over half a million inhabitants. Industries line the Seine from Argenteuil to Asnières, dominated by automobile and chemical factories. This heavily industrialized belt continues across the plain of Saint-Denis to Aubervilliers through the largest concentration of nineteenth-century industrialization in the agglomeration. Power

E. Kay

Photo 2. View westwards along the 'axis of tertiary activity' from the Palais de Chaillot across the Bois de Boulogne to the new commercial centre of La Défense in the background.

residential area of Neuilly constitutes an axis of tertiary activity which is rapidly becoming a westward extension of the central business district of the city. The main planning problems concern the overall incoherence of the physical structure, but the La Défense scheme together with the university and *préfecture* of Nanterre now give a clear nodal focus for future planning.

The eastern inner suburbs display a marked transition from a heavily industrialized northern section in Pantin and Bobigny, which shares many of the renewal problems of Aubervilliers, through a large area where smaller-scale industry and residences are intermingled, to the southern high quality residential suburbs of Vincennes and Saint-Mandé. Other than renewal, the main problems are the lack of large centres of tertiary employment and business activity, the loss of many industrial firms through closure or decentralization, and thus the high dependence on commuting to work.

In the southern inner suburbs the industrialized zone is much narrower than to the north of Paris. Manufacturing is mixed haphazardly with housing in the south-west, in Issy-les-Moulineaux, Vanves, and Malakoff, and also extends along the Seine valley. The southern fringe has witnessed much new building since the war, a notable example being Créteil, virtually a new town and now the *préfecture* of Val-de-Marne. Once again, planning problems concern the incoherence of functional organization of land uses and the vast daily journey to work movement.

Overall the inner suburban zone is characterized by its dependence on industrial employment and its mainly modest housing when examined from the point of view of density and quality. Much post-war building has been in the form of high density apartment complexes filling in the remaining open spaces. The zone is also characterized by the incoherence of its organization, with few strong suburban nodes and inadequate provision of public services. The latter point is particularly serious in relation to public transport. Although the inner suburbs lack the heavy congestion of the city, nevertheless they constitute the sector of Paris with the greatest levels of mobility. Commuters move in very large numbers to central Paris, particularly from the east and south, while a compensating current of commuters comes from both the city and the outer suburbs to industrial employment. The inner suburbs are beyond the reach of the Métro system and although public transport connection with central Paris is well developed albeit congested, movement between the suburbs is difficult.

generation, metallurgy, heavy engineering, and chemical industries were established alongside the railways and canals bringing coal from the north. The main planning problem is thus the poor quality of the urban environment, much of which is disfigured by old industries and containing areas, like Aubervilliers, in urgent need of physical renewal. It is also a zone lacking in coherent structure, with Saint-Denis the only focal point of importance.

The western inner suburbs share with those of the north a band of heavy industrialization lining the banks of the Seine, but away from the river land use is predominantly residential. A major feature is the development scheme of La Défense, which together with the adjacent high quality

The outer suburban ring

The outer suburbs are differentiated from the inner ring by the lack of total contiguity and continuity of the built-up area, the later age of development, and the highly active growth taking place at the present time. Their total population is approaching that of the inner suburbs but is expanding much more rapidly. This growth is mainly by migration not only from other regions of France but also from the centre of Paris, but the youthful age structure implies high rates of natural increase in the future.

A wide variety of landscapes is found in the outer suburbs. Between the two world wars a wave of speculative development, particularly along railway lines, created vast tracts of unco-ordinated and unplanned detached residences, the *lotissements*, which encircled the inner industrial suburbs. Since the Second World War suburban extension has consisted most typically of high-density apartment complexes, the so-called *cités* and *grands ensembles*—several, like Sarcelles, having populations equivalent to medium-sized towns. The rapid spread of suburbs along routeways has absorbed many pre-existing towns, such as Evry, Corbeil-Essonnes, Versailles, Pontoise, and Saint-Germain-en-Laye, into the agglomeration. Nevertheless the outer suburban ring is by no means completely urbanized and much open land, including extensive forests, remains undeveloped.

Although the outer suburbs discharge an enormous volume of commuters to central Paris they are far from being exclusively residential. Several factors account for the large and increasing amount of employment within the zone. First many major public utilities are located here, notably the airports of Orly and Le Bourget, and the new food market of Rungis. Secondly, the outer suburbs include many industries, particularly new growth industries, decentralized from central Paris and located on purpose-built estates served by good communications. This process has been particularly marked in the Seine Valley downstream towards Poissy, and upstream towards Evry. It is also marked in a new industrial belt extending from Rungis and Orly, through Massy and Antony, and along the valleys of the Bièvre and the Yvette. This decentralization not only of industry but also of educational and research establishments to the south and south-west of Paris is, together with the shift of industry downstream west of Paris, the major force shaping suburban extension at present. The construction of the new airport north of Paris will inevitably generate similar expansion in that direction. Growth eastwards along the Marne valley is also active but is predominantly residential. The lack of employment growth here, added to the deficit in the inner suburbs, confirms the east of the agglomeration as the greatest reservoir of commuters and points to a fundamental lack of equilibrium in the agglomeration as a whole.

The planning problems of the outer suburbs are crucial in view of the speed of development and the impact on the morphology of the entire agglomeration. The main risk is of anarchic growth causing Paris to spill out like a pool of oil and leading to further congestion. To avoid this, growth must be structured within planned zones and commuting reduced by rational location of employment. Pressure too is being placed not only on agricultural land but also on the remaining natural amenities of forest and water increasingly valuable for recreation. In response to these problems, the outer suburban zone is the location of planned new town development which aims to secure balanced expansion in relation to the entire agglomeration.

Each of the three major zones of Paris has its specific planning problem: decongestion of the centre, renewal and remodelling in the inner suburbs, and the need for a rational structure for the very rapid growth in the outer suburbs. These are not, however, separate problems for they are intricately interwoven in a functional sense and thus demand an integrated approach to the problems of the entire agglomeration.

Planning problems outside the agglomeration

The modern growth of Paris has conferred both advantages and disadvantages on the remainder of the Paris Basin. One undoubted advantage has been the focussing of routes through the Basin converging on Paris, giving it the densest transport network in France. Although the radial pattern does not make for easy transverse communications, nevertheless no part of the Basin can be considered as remote or isolated from easy means of transport. Similarly, the impetus of growth in Paris has spilled out into the Basin in the form of a stimulus to both agriculture and certain types of manufacturing to supply the Capital's needs. In recent years this impetus has been expressed in the form of industrial decentralization from Paris, creating much new employment in the towns of the Basin.

Against these advantages may be set serious disadvantages. In a real sense the feudal relationship of the past is perpetuated in the present. From the

TABLE 2
Population of the major agglomerations of the Paris Basin, 1968

Rouen	369 793	Bourges	76 088
Le Havre	247 374	Saint-Quentin	70 729
Tours	201 556	Creil	66 546
Reims	167 830	Charleville-Mézières	63 855
Orléans	167 515	Chartres	59 354
Le Mans	166 182	Mantes	57 893
Caen	152 332	Melun	57 179
Amiens	136 713	Châlons-sur-Marne	56 627
Troyes	114 209	Châteauroux	55 523
Cherbourg	79 121	Nevers	54 716

early nineteenth century onwards Paris drained the Basin of population to support her economic growth. This was an advantage in terms of successfully redeploying surplus agricultural population displaced by mechanization, and rural artisans whose livelihood was compromised by factory production techniques. However, this process undermined the position of the regional centres by eroding the population density of their hinterlands and restricting the development of their economies. This stifling of the regional centres is revealed by reference to their population totals.

Although the Paris Basin has an even distribution of urban centres (Fig. 1), Table 2 indicates that only nine agglomerations exceeded 100 000 inhabitants in 1968, and in an area accounting for over one-quarter of France, only twenty agglomerations of over 50 000 inhabitants are to be found. Only Rouen approaches the magnitude of a regional capital, and almost all the remaining centres are simply medium-sized towns with a localized sphere of influence. There is thus a major lack of equilibrium in the pattern of urbanization between the national capital, with an excessive concentration of population and activity, and insufficiently developed regional centres, which although relatively prosperous are not able to direct and animate the economies of their tributary regions adequately. It is significant in this respect that until very recently in this area only one university, at Caen, existed outside Paris.

The impetus of Paris towards industrialization has also been a qualified asset in the past. The impetus was most commonly applied to basic industries supplying the mundane needs of Paris in terms of energy supplies, foodstuffs, building materials, and semi-finished goods. Some of these industries, such as textiles, are now experiencing a contraction in employment; others, like wood-and leather-working are relatively stable; other activities, for example food processing, while expanding in output are stable in employment as a result of improved mechanization. Many other activities dependent on the Paris market, such as the processing of building materials, involve only semi-skilled labour and a low added-value. The basic industries of initial refining and processing, located for the most part at Le Havre and Rouen and involving petroleum, petrochemicals, and heavy chemicals, are capital intensive and thus employ small amounts of labour. They do on the other hand produce a high level of atmospheric pollution.

The direct impact of Paris is most marked within the core of the Basin, where agricultural land is being lost to the development of housing, motorways, and the new Paris-Nord airport, and where the degree of traffic congestion is constantly increasing, settlements are assuming dormitory functions, and recreational areas are coming under pressure. As compared with the negative influence of Paris alluded to in connection with the restricted development of regional centres in the peripheral zone, the influence here is both active and immediate. The resultant problems are essentially technical in that planning must seek to structure development so as to permit indispensable growth while maintaining the quality of the environment.

The recent trend, accentuated by deliberate government encouragement, for industry to decentralize from Paris, is now beginning to transform the Paris Basin. From being a suppressor of growth in the regional centres, Paris has begun to act as a generator of new growth. While no rapid change in the fundamental disequilibrium of urbanization can be effected, nevertheless most of the towns of the Paris Basin are currently experiencing rapid population growth, related in many instances to the acquisition of industries decentralized from Paris.

The growth rate of the Paris agglomeration between 1962 and 1968 was approximately 8 per cent, roughly the same as that of the nation as a whole. Table 3 shows that this was vastly exceeded by almost all the agglomerations of the Paris Basin —in most cases by a substantial margin. The most rapid growth rates, of over 30 per cent, have been achieved by towns in close proximity to Paris. In fact Mantes, Creil, and Melun are virtually annexes of the central agglomeration and their growth is inseparable from it. At the other extreme, a number of towns on the fringe of the Paris Basin, such as Charleville-Mézières, Cherbourg, Châteauroux, and Nevers, have experienced much slower growth. This reflects in part their greater distance from Paris and inability to attract decentralized firms and also the decline of their traditional economic activities.

Between these two extremes it is apparent that most of the larger centres of the Basin have grown rapidly, and that much of this growth may be attributed to migrational gain. This is a welcome trend in that it is providing the Basin with a net-work of growth centres capable of stemming the drift of population to Paris, but it has implied rapid physical expansion in towns unaccustomed to change at such speed. This presents serious planning problems, as historic city centres become immured behind mushrooming apartment complexes, the transport systems become strained, and public services and administration have to adjust to new dimensions. These problems are posed with particular severity in a limited number of locations where the pattern of urban growth has been linear, following major transport alignments. The outstanding case is the Basse-Seine area, the corridor linking Paris via Rouen to Le Havre. Although both Rouen and Le Havre are shown by Table 3 to have grown at a slower rate than many other centres, because of their large populations their absolute growth in numbers is very great, and their potential for further growth undoubted. In these circumstances, there is a need for an overall structure plan for urban and economic development in the Basse-Seine, in order to prevent piecemeal and anarchic growth leading to a virtual axis of urbanization joined to Paris, with resultant problems of congestion,

TABLE 3

Population change in the major agglomerations 1962–8

Agglomeration	Rate of change per cent	Migration rate per cent	Distance from Paris in kilometres
Mantes	38·5	28·5	60
Creil	36·7	29·2	50
Melun	29·3	19·8	45
Caen	25·8	16·6	227
Tours	22·5	16·8	235
Châlons-sur-Marne	22·1	13·1	160
Chartres	21·4	14·8	94
Orléans	18·7	11·8	115
Reims	16·8	10·3	154
Bourges	16·7	11·6	224
Le Mans	14·0	6·2	215
Troyes	13·4	7·9	160
Rouen	12·7	5·3	140
Amiens	12·7	5·7	131
Nevers	10·5	6·4	236
Charleville-Mézières	10·2	2·6	237
Cherbourg	9·6	1·6	346
Le Havre	9·5	3·4	226
Saint-Quentin	6·9	1·0	140
Châteauroux	5·0	−1·0	251

Photo 3. Rouen, a major regional centre in the Paris Basin. In the foreground, the historic core; on the skyline, apartment complexes testifying to new growth

pollution and environmental destruction. Similar problems on a smaller scale apply to the lower Oise Valley between Compiègne and Pontoise.

This chapter has attempted merely to identify problems in terms of their general character and their spatial characteristics. No attempt has been made to give a detailed analysis since this is more appropriate to the following chapter which seeks to review the underlying causes of the planning problems summarized above.

2 The Causes of Problems

Most of the problems confronting Paris have not appeared overnight but by a process of evolution, at first gradual and then accelerating. An explanation of the causes of problems is therefore best achieved by a chronological approach.

The growth of Paris to 1850

Only vestiges remain of the initial left bank site of Paris for after numerous attacks the settlement was rebuilt on the more secure Ile de la Cité. For several centuries the greater part of the town was confined to the island, but throughout the Middle Ages a gradual extension took place on both banks. By the end of the twelfth century when the first external walls were built, Paris sheltered approximately 200 000 inhabitants and had a basic tripartite structure. The Ile de la Cité remained the centre of power as manifest in the palaces of the king and the bishop. The right bank had developed as the commercial and artisan quarter, inhabited by merchants, traders, and the workers in small-scale industries who used the Seine for both transport and water power. On the left bank religious institutions grew as centres of learning, leading to a general burgeoning of intellectual life.

From this compact nucleus, Paris expanded in a broadly concentric fashion until the middle of the nineteenth century. This was achieved through the successive enlargement of the line of fortifications, which nevertheless displayed a preference for growth on the right bank. This reflected the physical ease of expansion across the valley floor and between low cols in the ranges of hills enclosing the valley to the north, as compared with the more constricting relief to the south. The site advantages of the right bank were complemented by its greater commercial importance and its choice as the location for royal palaces. By the outbreak of the Revolution, the population of Paris had increased to over half a million and to accommodate this growth the walls had been extended four times. When the last fortifications were built in 1841, the population had increased to approximately one million and the city had expanded far beyond the confines of the valley floor.

The legacy of the period of concentric growth to 1850 lies, in terms of present planning problems, in the congested nature of the heart of the city. The effort to confine the city within its walls produced a medieval street pattern characterized by a high density of narrow streets laid out in a rectilinear plan. The exceptions are the elliptical boulevards built on the lines of the demolished walls, together with the more spacious boulevards built later by Haussman. The preservation of this dense street pattern has given central Paris a structure within which congestion of traffic and buildings was inevitable. A further legacy is the lack of a spirit of urbanism in the period up to 1850. The city grew through a haphazard spilling of population outside the existing walls, followed by annexation and a subsequent enlargement of the fortified perimeter. The main effort of State and public endeavour was in the form of magnificent monuments but no tradition of civic planning had been established. Finally, by 1850, the phenomenon of rigid centralization had been firmly established, initially through the monarchy and then even more comprehensively after the Revolution, by the State.

The railway era and its aftermath

In the second half of the nineteenth century two major changes were to alter the entire growth process of the agglomeration and introduce a new range of problems. First the effort to restrain Paris within fortifications was abandoned in view of their irrelevance to modern warfare, and secondly the arrival of railway transport gave an opportunity to exploit this new freedom to expand. As compared with the past concentric development, Paris now entered a phase of radial or tentacular growth guided by the railway lines.

The railways emanated from termini within the 1841 fortifications and were essentially designed to link the Capital with the Provinces. The suburbs thus followed the railways rather than the railways being planned to serve the suburbs. The resultant urban morphology was star-shaped, the tentacles being more pronounced south of the Seine, where the plateau margin of Beauce interposed a barrier and confined the railways to the valleys. Coincident with the railway era was also the onset of the Industrial Revolution, converting Paris from being primarily a producer of de luxe articles to being the largest and most diversified industrial city of France.

The latter half of the nineteenth century wit-

Photo 4. The problem of urban renewal in the industrial suburbs: decayed housing in St Denis

nessed an enormous suburban extension beyond the limits of 1841. This extension assumed two main forms. First, an inner ring consisting of industrial suburbs with a proletarian population developed around Paris. Factories sought level land served by rail and canal—conditions fulfilled to the north of Paris on the plain of Saint-Denis and westwards along the Seine valley. Secondly, suburban extension of a predominantly residential character followed the railway lines radiating from Paris and gave birth to the phenomenon of commuting. Suburban extension was the inevitable result of explosive population growth as migrants flocked to employment in Paris. Between 1860 and the close of the century the population doubled to approximately 4 million in the agglomeration as a whole.

During this phase of explosive suburban growth some remodelling of the city centre took place due to the efforts of Haussman, Prefect of Paris from 1853 to 1870. His main concern was to open up the city centre by driving broad boulevards through the built-up area and demolishing in the process many areas of poorer housing which were cores of political unrest. Thus a great north–south boulevard was created through the heart of the city crossing the Ile de la Cité, together with a series of arcuate boulevards on both banks linking the Place de l'Étoile with the Place de la Bastille. Vast new intersections were created at the Étoile, Madeleine, Opéra and Trocadéro, which have since become major foci of traffic and points of congestion. Imposing though Haussman's works were, it must be pointed out that they concerned only the city centre and no comparable effort was made in the suburbs where the most dynamic growth was taking place. Moreover, the motivation was essentially strategic in terms of controlling the population, rather than an attempt to improve the quality of the urban environment as a whole.

The incessant growth of population continued into the twentieth century and by 1920 the agglomeration had acquired 5 million inhabitants. In the period between the world wars, the physical expansion of suburbs reached new dimensions with the exploitation of *lotissements*. These were vast tracts of land acquired by individual speculators or private companies which, with the spread of railway transport and the private vehicle, assumed enormous value. Land was sold for development, often with little consolidation into rational building plots and with only a rudimentary provision of roads and services. The result was the appearance in a very short period of time of enormous suburban tracts of low-density housing, very largely dependent for employment on central Paris but located progressively further from the centre.

By 1935 the agglomeration had attained a popu-

Photo 5. The *grand ensemble* of Sarcelles

I.A.U.R.P.

lation of approximately 6 million, of which only 2·8 million resided within the city proper. The main changes in the city were concerned with improving transport. The demolition of the 1841 walls after the First World War permitted the creation of an exterior boulevard around the city. Similarly circulation within Paris was eased by the creation of the Métro underground system, inaugurated in 1900.

Some of the most serious problems facing the agglomeration were inherited from the century of tentacular growth after 1850. Above all it was during this time that Paris assumed its enormous size in terms both of population and of physical extent. By the opening of the Second World War Paris had been transformed from a populous but compact city into a sprawling metropolis. The *lotissements* bequeathed a legacy of vast undistinguished suburbs, underequipped in terms of facilities and subject to weak administration. The period also marked a great increase in the separation of place of residence from place of work with a consequent increase in the number of commuters using transport systems ill-adapted to meet such demands.

In particular the underground system was largely confined to the city and did not reach out into the suburbs. To the north and north-west of the city proletarian industrial suburbs had burgeoned which now are in need of renewal. Finally,

the expansion of the suburbs took place in a *laissez-faire* manner unrestrained by effective planning measures. As a result there was a lack of nodular development in the outer suburbs—of service centres and concentrations of employment —capable of reducing the strains imposed on the city centre.

Expansion since 1945

During the depression years the population growth of Paris declined significantly. The war years perpetuated this tendency and until 1954 expansion of the agglomeration was restrained, and the amount of new building relatively small. After 1954 a new wave of growth began, swollen by migration but sustained by a large and unexpected rise in the natural increase of the population. The immediate result was a critical housing shortage brought about by the lack of new building and by the conversion of residential property to commercial functions in central Paris. At the same time rapid industrial expansion produced a demand for land as firms seeking to expand searched for new sites away from the congested centre and inner suburbs. The inevitable result was an infilling of the agglomeration and particularly of the interstices between the main suburban tentacles. Unlike the earlier extensive pattern of the *lotissements*, the shortage of land near to the centre and the resultant high price of building land led to an emphasis on high-density development in collective schemes of apartment blocks. These were commonly of such dimensions as to form *cités* with several thousand inhabitants and with a tendency to grow more rapidly than the necessary amenities. This process culminated in the creation of *grands ensembles*: vast housing complexes with the dimensions of towns but with only modest social and administrative provision. The case may be cited of Sarcelles, on the northern fringe of the agglomeration, which grew from 8397 inhabitants in 1954 to 35 430 in 1962.

The result of the process of infilling was that by the mid 1960s Paris once more had assumed a concentric morphology with, at the same time, a further generation of commuters contributing to the strangulation of Paris. By 1965 the population of the agglomeration had attained 8 million with every indication of rapid growth continuing.

Since the mid 1960s, the expansion of Paris has indeed continued and by 1970 the population reached a total of 8·5 million in the agglomeration. It is significant that the emphasis in population growth has passed from a dominant role of migration to a position where 70 per cent of the growth was due to natural increase. This in part reflects a slowing down in industrial employment growth consequent on decentralization, and partly the greater vigour of urban expansion in the Provinces, both trends leading to a reduction in the stream of migrants to Paris. The main internal changes have taken place in the sphere of transport with the construction of intra-urban motorways in the form of a ring motorway, the *Boulevard Périphérique* built outside the 1841 fortifications line, and an expressway, partly underground, on the right bank of the Seine. Together with the completion of inter-urban motorways radiating from Paris to north, south and west, this has given a stimulus to commuting by car from greater and greater distances. In this there is a parallel with the effect of railways a century earlier in that the motorways encourage once more tentacular development radially from Paris. The motorway interchanges are the present-day equivalent of the suburban railway stations but the efficiency in terms of mass transit is substantially lower.

The planning problems which have accrued from post-war growth are chiefly differentiated from those of past periods by their dimensions. The difficulties of living and working in the agglomeration now involve more people and extend over a wider area than ever before. The most obvious expression of this is to be found in the growth of commuting. Suburban extension has resulted in an increasing separation of place of work from place of residence and over 900 000 workers now travel daily from the suburbs to employment in Paris. This total is increasing by approximately 20 000 per annum. A further 200 000 persons travel from Paris to jobs in the suburbs. In addition to this commuting to and from central Paris, over half a million persons are involved in journey to work movements between suburbs. Moreover, a large proportion of the working inhabitants of central Paris must cross the city to their employment, sharing the same congested transport systems as the longer-distance commuters. The results of this massive and complex pattern of daily movement to work are the imposition of fatigue, loss of time, and a manifest tendency for improvements in the efficiency of transport systems to be overtaken by the growth in demand.

The pattern of the daily movement of the agglomeration's 3-million-strong work-force can be divided into two main categories. Approximately half of the movements are from suburb to suburb or from central Paris to employment in the suburbs. Over 60 per cent of these journeys involve private transport by car or motorized cycle, the majority of the remainder either working *in situ* or travelling short distances on foot. The predominance of private vehicles reflects in part the paucity of inter-suburban public transport, the relatively short distance travelled on average, and in the case of movement from Paris to the suburbs, the preponderance of managerial class workers with a high level of car ownership. In most instances the journey to work is completed within half an hour. By contrast, the remaining half of the working population, involved in journeys to work from the suburbs to Paris or from one district to another within central Paris, rely approximately 80 per cent on public transport. In the case of suburban commuters, this invariably implies a change in mode of transport from suburban train to Métro or bus. The main railway termini and their associated Métro stations thus become the focal points of congestion during the rush hours. The suburban commuter is thus most prone to problems of fatigue, delays and overcrowding, the time spent travelling to work averaging one and a half hours daily.

Over 10 per cent of all commuters to central Paris travel by private vehicle and the proportion is growing constantly. Access to central Paris has been improved by the extension of motorways and expressways, but within Paris the problems of congestion, difficulties of parking, and increased atmospheric pollution are becoming more serious. In total, from both social and economic standpoints, the problem of commuting has become a crucial planning issue. The attendant problems of the high cost of improving transport systems, the expropriation of land for road construction, and the growth of noise and atmospheric pollution make this the most sensitive and controversial planning problem in the entire agglomeration. It has been calculated that each day the Paris Region generates 12·2 million journeys by private and public transport. Since at present trends the level of private car ownership is expected to double in the Region by 1985, the problem of circulation is certain to remain crucial into the foreseeable future. Clearly solutions are to be found not only in improvements in transport systems, but in the more rational location of activities—closer to the source of commuters.

The problem of accommodating the much increased post-war population of the agglomeration has been eased by the mushrooming of *grands ensembles*, but the latter in turn have created new strains. The high density of living accommodation, the predominance of young families, the underdevelopment of social and recreational amenities, especially in the earlier complexes, tended to produce an environment lacking true urban character or community life. The fact that such major complexes are commonly located far from important employment centres and often have deficient transport connections means that they disgorge large numbers of commuters, many of whom travel by private car. The adoption of industrialized building techniques applied to the creation of huge estates has provided a great increase in the stock of relatively inexpensive housing in the agglomeration, but this does not conceal the fact that a large proportion of the total population is badly housed. Meanwhile the task of the renewal of the old quarters of central Paris and sections of the inner industrial suburbs remains urgent. Similarly the need to decentralize activity from the congested centre continues to be a serious problem, although major efforts have been made in the case of industrial employment.

A further problem which has been aggravated in the post-war period is the loss of agricultural land and open spaces before the advancing tide of urbanization. The loss of land with high amenity value, such as woodland and waterside land is a serious problem, since this comes about at a time when the pressures of fatigue and of high-density housing with few amenities place a premium on easy access to open land for recreation.

Above all, by the mid 1960s the need for an integrated approach to the planning of economic activity and the physical use of land throughout the entire agglomeration was abundantly clear, as was the need for an appropriate administrative and planning structure for this process.

The lack of planning

Many of the more serious aspects of the problems cited in this and the previous chapter would be less serious had the growth of Paris been subject to some measure of control and planning. In fact the expansion of the agglomeration has until very recently taken place in a generally *laissez-faire* manner, haphazard growth being interspersed with periodic and generally ineffective attempts to control and organize the sprawl. In particular the suburban extension during the last hundred years has proceeded in an anarchic fashion. The failure to achieve a rational urban structure stems from administrative fragmentation resulting from the spread of the agglomeration across numerous local government units located in several separate *départements*, the financial weakness of the individual municipalities which retarded infrastructure developments, and the limited legal powers which could be invoked to plan comprehensively.

At the turn of the last century awareness of the acute housing shortage and of the general deterioration of the housing stock stimulated a number of government inquiries, but action was impeded by the outbreak of the First World War. The wave of speculative building after 1920 highlighted the need for a general development plan, and in 1928 a planning authority was created for this purpose, 'Le Comité Supérieur de l'Aménagement et l'Organisation Générale de la Région Parisienne', (C.A.R.P.). It was a decade before this authority produced, and the government approved, a comprehensive plan, the Prost–Dausset Plan of 1939. This applied to an area within a 35-kilometre radius of the cathedral of Notre-Dame but excluded the city proper, which was considered to be entirely urbanized and adequately serviced. The objective of the plan was to restrain further piecemeal development of *lotissements* by the designation of building zones outside which construction was prohibited. Open spaces were to be created, new radial roads built, and limits on building height imposed. In fact little was achieved under this plan other than the commencement of the *Autoroute de l'Ouest* and some improvements to public services in the *lotissements*. War once more intervened and in the post-war decade priority was attached to restoring war damage, which amounted to 27 000 dwellings and 300 factories destroyed. Moreover, official expectation was that the growth of Paris, which had shown some deceleration in the pre-war decade, would be of modest proportions in the future.

It was clear by 1955 that this appraisal was false, for between 1946 and 1954 the agglomeration increased by 600 000 inhabitants and a new generation of the homeless and badly-housed was added to a city already suffering a backlog of slum clearance. Forceful government measures involving the financing of low-rent collective housing were enacted but the prospect of new suburbs on such a large scale and at such a high density pointed even more emphatically to the urgent need for a comprehensive physical plan for the agglomeration. Accordingly in 1956 the preparation of such a master plan, 'Le Plan d'Aménagement et d'Organisation Générale de la Région Parisienne' (P.A.D.O.G.), was set in motion.

The P.A.D.O.G. proposals received government approval in 1960 and concerned the period 1960 to 1970. During this time-span an increase in population of one million inhabitants was forecast, which, it was considered, could be accommodated within the limits of the existing agglomeration. The crux of the plan was essentially to restrain employment growth by encouraging industrial and office decentralization and to accommodate population increase by infilling the agglomeration, in turn made more viable by improved transport and massive urban renewal. The major transport proposals were the creation of two trunk ring roads, the *Boulevard Périphérique* and the *Autoroute Interurbaine de Seine et Oise* (A.R.I.S.O.), while the urban renewal proposals envisaged the establishment of strong urban nodes within the amorphous and disorganized suburban zone.

The P.A.D.O.G. plan may be criticized, with the benefit of hindsight, on the basis of the relatively short-term time scale involved, which encouraged a search for palliatives rather than fundamental solutions. The assumption that economic and population growth could and should be restrained now appears dubious, and the lack of integration between the agglomeration and the wider city region was unrealistic. Nevertheless the P.A.D.O.G. proposals were an advance in the right direction and formed the basis of important decisions, notably in the spheres of transport and in the initiation of the suburban node of La Défense. Moreover, the plan should not be seen in isolation from other reforms initiated during the 1960s which helped to prepare the ground for a more ambitious attack on the planning problems of the Paris Region.

In 1961 the *District de la Région Parisienne* was created, encompassing the existing *départements* of Seine, Seine-et-Oise, and Seine-et-Marne. The District is not a territorial unit but a public body associating the various local authorities which would otherwise plan individually. The *District* thus assures co-ordination and integration in the effort of physical planning and public investment. Administrative reform was carried a stage further in 1964 when the *départements* of Seine and Seine-et-Oise, which with a combined population of almost 8 million inhabitants had functioned with increasing difficulty, were subdivided into seven new *départements* (Fig. 2). This reform had the double advantage of bringing administration more closely into contact with the population, and by the creation of new *préfectures* of providing strong focal points within the previously anonymous suburban sprawl.

The regional framework for planning was strengthened in 1966 by the formal institution of planning regions in the nation as a whole. The Paris Region constituted one of these twenty-one regions, headed by a Regional Prefect who also holds the position of head executive of the Paris District. The prime responsibility of the Prefect is to implement government economic and social policy, as determined by the National Plans, within the Paris Region. By 1966, therefore, an institutional framework had been forged for the application of planning that was integrated throughout the agglomeration through the medium of the Paris District, and that was regional in context through the mechanism of the Regional Prefect's administration. By 1966, one of the chief causes of serious difficulties in the Paris agglomeration—the absence of effective planning machinery—had been removed and the ground had been prepared for a vigorous and long-term assault on the problems of the agglomeration and its tributary region.

3 Planning Strategy

The planned attack on the problems of the Paris Basin has been based on three main fronts. Policies have been designed to redress the balance between Paris and provincial France. Action has been taken within the agglomeration to promote a more rational organization of population, economic activity, and administration. Plans have also been announced to secure a more balanced development throughout the Paris Basin. These three strategies were initially developed to meet separate and distinctive problems, but a growing realization of their interrelationship has resulted in a co-ordination of effort in recent years. As a result there now exists an integrated approach to planning in the Paris Basin, guided by overall objectives and principles.

Paris and the Provinces

Measures to minimize the economic and social disparities between Paris and the remainder of the country have been in operation since 1955. These have taken the form of decentralization policies, aimed at restricting industrial development in Paris and encouraging investment in the Provinces. Secondly, since 1965 a deliberate attempt has been made to develop the provincial capitals as effective metropolitan centres, capable of counterbalancing the weight of Paris.

Industrial decentralization

Industrial decentralization policies were intended to fulfil the double role of decongesting Paris and channelling new investment towards regions in serious need of economic growth. On the one hand the closure of factories in Paris releases land for priority developments such as housing and transport, while the installation of new factories in the Provinces assists the task of reducing the gap in employment opportunities between Paris and certain critical regions. Specifically, the old-established industrial areas, as in the cases of the northern coalfield and the Lorraine steel district, are suffering a contraction of their staple industries and are in urgent need of diversification. More generally, the whole of western France is under-industrialized and in need of new activity to raise income levels, check out-migration, and transfer surplus rural population into more productive employment.

Decentralization policy began simply in 1949 with aid to areas of high industrial unemployment, but has now evolved into a highly complex system of controls and incentives. Industry is now discouraged from expansion in Paris by a system of building permits involving penalty payments levied on additional factory floorspace created, while a system of grants is provided for new industrial investment in the Provinces. In some instances, permission to extend factories in Paris has been conditional on the creation of new plant in priority development regions. Fig. 5 shows that the generosity of government aid to industry is proportional to the severity of the needs of a particular area. Thus four major zones are favoured by the government. The whole of western and central France benefits from development grants towards the cost of installing plant and from certain tax exemptions. A discontinuous zone in the east, including the traditional heavy industrial areas where staple activities are shedding labour, benefits from conversion grants to firms whose activities help to diversify the industrial structure. A third fragmented zone in eastern France including many smaller towns

Fig. 5. Government aid to industry

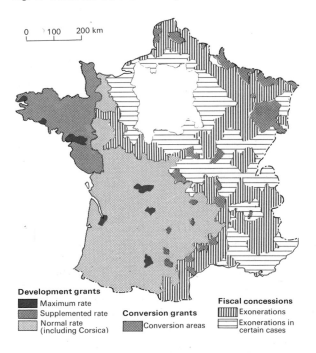

0   100   200 km

Development grants
■ Maximum rate
▨ Supplemented rate
□ Normal rate (including Corsica)

Conversion grants
▨ Conversion areas

Fiscal concessions
▥ Exonerations
▤ Exonerations in certain cases

receives tax exemptions for new industrial investment. The remainder of the country, with the exception of the core of the Paris Basin, qualifies for tax concessions to a lesser extent. In addition to this direct financial aid, the government also provides indirect aid in the form of labour retraining schemes, funds for establishing industrial estates, and grants towards the cost of relocating machinery.

In terms of its objectives, the policy of decentralization has had mixed success. Up to 1968 over 2500 decentralization moves from the Paris Region had received government aid, the peak being 289 operations in 1961. In the years between 1955 and 1959 it was noticeable that most decentralizations were to locations relatively close to Paris, mainly within a 200 kilometre radius. Between 1959 and 1962 the number of operations increased and the proportion of long distance decentralizations to the under-developed regions also increased. Since 1962, however, the number of operations has fallen to little more than 100 per annum and the preference for locations relatively close to Paris has reappeared. These latest trends reflect the fact that most of the large firms susceptible to decentralization have now completed the operation, while many of the remaining smaller firms are too closely linked to component and ancillary industries in Paris to contemplate decentralization. Recent transfers have consisted mainly of movement from the central city and inner suburbs to the periphery of the agglomeration or to towns within the immediate orbit of Paris. A further weakness of the process is that whereas a large number of jobs have been suppressed in manufacturing, these tend to be outweighed by the creation of new employment in the remaining industry in spite of government restrictions, and by the continued growth of office employment. Moreover, most decentralization operations have consisted of the establishment of subsidiary factories in the Provinces whilst the original factory in Paris has been retained. In comparatively few cases has a total decentralization involving the closure of the Paris factory and transfer of administration taken place. Nor have large movements of employees taken place. Decentralization has usually involved the transfer of key workers and management to new plants, but the bulk of the work force has remained in the Paris factories, or in the case of closure, has found alternative employment locally rather than leaving the Capital.

In spite of these limitations some success for the decentralization policy can be claimed in two respects. It has given some impetus to industrial development in the Provinces since one-fifth of all floorspace and one-eighth of the new industrial jobs created there may be attributed to one or other form of decentralization. Secondly, some decongestion of Paris has resulted even when the movement has only been as far as the periphery of the agglomeration. On the other hand, these partial successes have not been entirely to the benefit of Paris. The closure of factories tends to have been concentrated in eastern Paris, whereas the creation of new employment in both industry and the tertiary occupations has been to the west and south of the agglomeration, where motorways have been strong attractions. This has left the east with a deficit of activity and an excessive level of commuting. Also, a large number of smaller firms without the resources to contemplate decentralization find their operations hindered by government restrictions on expansion *in situ*.

Office decentralization

Since 1960 attempts have been made to decentralize tertiary activities, again with the double aim of aiding employment growth in the Provinces and of decongesting the heart of the agglomeration. In addition to control through planning permits, grants are given for the demolition of office buildings or for their conversion to other uses. As in industry penalties are levied against new office construction.

As a strategy, decentralization of office employment has had less success than in the case of industry. The dispersion has been over even shorter distances, usually from central Paris to the inner suburbs, and head offices have invariably remained rooted in the city even when ancillary services have been decentralized. In spite of penalties, central Paris has accounted for 35 per cent of new office employment in the agglomeration in recent years, and movement to the inner suburbs, such as Neuilly and the new business centre of La Défense, has accounted for over 40 per cent. A further type of movement has been that of research and educational establishments to the south of Paris, particularly to Orsay. A consequence of these selective trends has been once more to leave the eastern suburbs deficient in employment opportunities. In an attempt to redress this balance and also to encourage further dispersal of employment, the government is now moving towards a graduation of the penalties imposed on office construction, with the highest levies being imposed on the central business district and the western suburbs, and lower levels in the case of the eastern suburbs. Development may also be restrained in the north of the agglomeration so as to channel growth created by the new airport of Paris–Nord towards the east and the Marne Valley.

The regional metropolises

Apart from the wish to spread employment opportunities, the policy of office decentralization also aims to disseminate the power of decision more widely in the Provinces. One of the reasons for the reluctance of firms to move from Paris has been the limited powers of decision vested in the provincial centres. Since 1965 the government has attempted to alleviate this problem by the nomination of regional metropolises (Fig. 6). The function of these cities is to counterbalance the weight of Paris by improving their services and institutions and thus their capacity to attract both industrial firms and office development. The formation of such growth poles is being aided by priority investment in transport development, expansion of universities and surgical hospitals, and the expansion of industrial estates, housing

I.A.U.R.P.

Photo 6. Office decentralization to the inner suburbs: the new suburban node of La Défense

Fig. 6. The regional metropolises

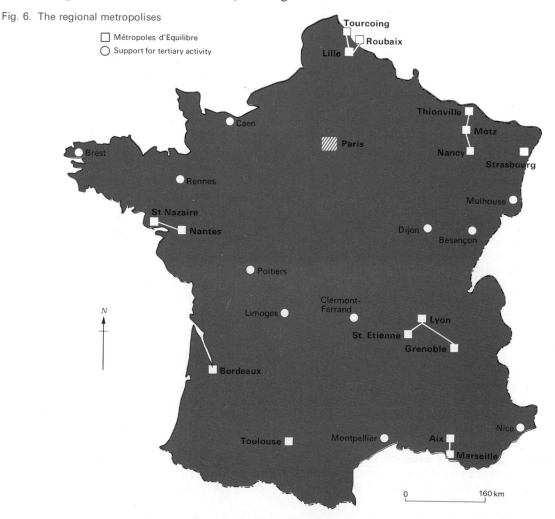

schemes, and office complexes. It is hoped that by enhancing the quality of service provision an atmosphere will be created conducive to an intensification of commercial and business activity and cultural life, enabling the metropolises to fulfil a role as genuine regional capitals. For this to be successful, some devolution of power from Paris, both in regional administration and in business organization, is clearly desirable in order to achieve a measure of independence from the Capital. Some of the selected metropolises, notably Lyon, Marseille, Toulouse and Grenoble, have enjoyed considerable spontaneous growth, but others, such as Nantes, Lille, Bordeaux and Nancy, do not as yet have a comparable credibility as future strong regional capitals. A number of smaller centres have also been selected as priority areas for decentralization of tertiary employment on a lesser scale (Fig. 6).

The strategies described above, aimed at creating a more equitable balance between the Capital and the Provinces while at the same time easing the pressure of congestion in Paris, have as their counterpart far-reaching plans to reorganize the structure of the Paris agglomeration.

A strategy for Paris

The lack of a planning perspective has already been cited as a major cause of the outstanding problems of the Paris Region. The publication of the P.A.D.O.G. proposals in 1960 was thus a major landmark, but as early as 1963 important revisions were taking place and the assumption that growth could be contained within the existing agglomeration was being challenged. In particular, a revision of population growth estimates, forecasting a population of at least 12 million and possibly 16 million by the year 2000, encouraged the view that a planned extension of the agglomeration was inevitable. Against this expansionist background a thorough review was made leading to a master plan, the *Schéma Directeur,* in 1965.

Paris 2000—the *Schéma Directeur*

The proposals embodied in the *Schéma Directeur* must be evaluated in the light of the assumptions made in its preparation. The most important assumption was that the population would continue to grow rapidly, resulting in an additional 6 million inhabitants in the Paris Region by the close of the century. This assessment does not imply the acceptance of further parasitic growth by Paris, but on the contrary assumes that with active decentralization policies the regional metropolises and the main towns of the Paris Basin will triple their populations by the year 2000 and that the remaining urban centres will double theirs. A second assumption was a constant rise in prosperity and, as a result of increased affluence, a tripling of private vehicle ownership to over 5 millions. The volume of transport by all modes was expected to triple or even quadruple. With effective decentralization policies, the planners assumed that employment growth in manufacturing would increase by only 30 per cent from 2 million jobs to 2·7 million, while the volume of tertiary employment would almost double from 1·8 million to 3·4 million. It was further assumed that the amount of housing would almost double by the end of the century, to 6 million dwelling units. Taking into account improvements in environmental and design standards it was estimated that the total surface area occupied by industrial buildings would double, that of office buildings would triple, and that of residential occupation would quadruple in the Paris Region by the year 2000.

It is clear from these assumptions that the policy of containment, implicit in the P.A.D.O.G. proposals, would no longer serve as a strategy in the longer term and that a planned extension of the agglomeration was inescapable. The originality of the *Schéma Directeur* was in the form of extension adopted out of the numerous options considered. The possibility of a ring of new towns comparable with those developed around London was, for example, rejected as perpetuating the worst feature inherited from the past: that of concentric development leading to strangulation. Instead, the *Schéma Directeur* opted for development along two axes tangential to the outline of the existing agglomeration. Before describing in detail the character of the axes of development, it is important to recognize that the *Schéma Directeur* was not intended as a detailed blueprint but as a structure plan, a strategic decision on the main outlines for future growth. The essence of the plan was thus a map drawn at 1 : 100 000 scale, which zoned land according to the type and direction of development proposed. The detailed physical planning and phasing of expansion was delegated to smaller planning units and was contingent upon the evolution of economic, demographic, and financial considerations which are not amenable to forecasting at long range.

The preferential axes and new towns

The two preferential axes proposed in the *Schéma Directeur* are aligned roughly south-east and north-west for a distance of 75 kilometres in the case of the northern axis and 90 kilometres in the case of its southern counterpart. The basis of development along these axes is to be a combination of new town construction in the form of extensions to the agglomeration and major redevelopment schemes where the axes traverse the suburban zone of the existing agglomeration. The axes are also conceived as strong lines of movement, linking the new towns with each other and also, by rapid transit systems, with the centre of the agglomeration. Several advantages may be claimed for this strategy, most of all the fact that it attempts to halt the concentric expansion which has characterized the modern growth of Paris. Secondly, the fact that the axes extend through the agglomeration preserves the unity of the latter and in particular its integrity as a labour market. Thirdly, the orientation of the axes is such that land with high amenity value, particularly along the river valleys, can be conserved but at the same time be accessible from the new towns. Finally, the concentration of new housing along transport axes will permit some separation of through east–west traffic from the circulation taking place at the heart of the agglomeration and this implies reductions in investment costs in transport systems as compared with a more general and diffused suburban expansion.

The main elements of the 1965 *Schéma Directeur* are summarized in Fig. 7. The most striking proposals concern the creation of new towns and suburban redevelopment, which it was anticipated could accommodate approximately two-thirds of the estimated population increase to the year 2000.

In the case of the northern axis the *Schéma Directeur* proposed three new towns and two new urban centres. The plateau to the south-west of Pontoise was designated to receive a new town, Cergy-Pontoise, ultimately with over 300 000 inhabitants. The axis continues eastwards across the valley of Montmorency, chosen as the site of a second new town, Beauchamp. In addition, redeveloped centres were proposed for St. Denis and Stains, and a university for Villetaneuse, bringing new facilities to a suburban area at present badly serviced. The new town together with suburban redevelopment would, it was estimated, house a further 600 000 inhabitants in the north of the agglomeration. Continuing eastwards, the opening of the new airport of Paris–Nord and the creation of over 30 000 related jobs will add new vigour to the north-eastern suburbs. The *Schéma* considered that because of noise, new development should be at some distance from

Fig. 7. The *Schéma Directeur*

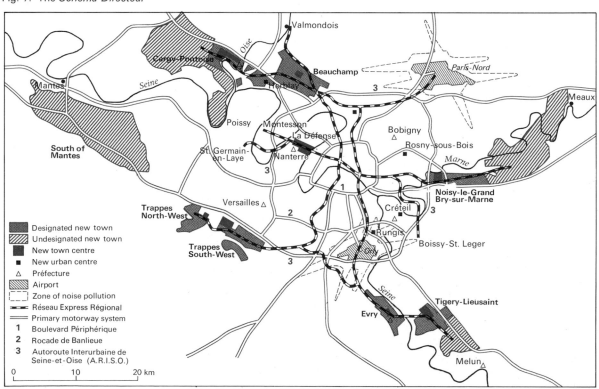

TABLE 4
Resident population in the proposed new towns

	1962	Estimate 1985	Forecast 2000
Northern Axis			
Cergy-Pontoise	40 000	130 000	700 000–1 000 000
Beauchamp	12 000	60 000	300 000– 500 000
Bry-sur-Marne	40 000	90 000	700 000–1 000 000
Southern Axis			
South of Mantes	1000	5000	300 000–400 000
Trappes South-east	3000	100 000	400 000–600 000
Trappes North-west	2000	100 000	300 000–400 000
Evry	7000	100 000	300 000–500 000
Tigery-Lieusaint	5000	35 000	400 000–600 000
Total	110 000	620 000	Approx. 4 500 000

the airport. The site of Le Bourget airport, to be closed when Paris–Nord is commissioned, was therefore designated for redevelopment as a major suburban employment node. The *préfecture* of the new *département* of Seine–St.-Denis, Bobigny, was selected as a node for redevelopment providing an administrative and commercial focus for the north-eastern suburbs. East of Paris, the northern axis follows the line of the Marne Valley linking the existing towns on the north bank as far as Meaux which already serve as dormitory suburbs. The *Schéma* proposed new town development on the left bank of the Marne which is as yet undeveloped. A chain of new towns, each of from 30 000 to 80 000 inhabitants was considered best-suited to the dissected relief and in total these could accommodate between 300 000 and 500 000 inhabitants. This complex would have as its focus a new urban centre, Bry-sur-Marne–Noisy-le-Grand, with commercial and university functions and also a new television broadcasting complex. Between this new town and Paris, a suburban redevelopment at Rosny-sous-Bois was considered necessary to enhance employment opportunities in the tertiary sector, at present insufficient in the eastern suburbs as we have seen.

The southern preferential axis begins south of Mantes, where the *Schéma* proposed a new town, the exact form being undesignated. The axis continues eastwards through a major zone of proposed new urbanization to the south-west of Versailles, based on two new town centres northwest and south-east of Trappes with a total population of 400 000 inhabitants. The southern axis terminates in the Seine Valley between Paris and Melun with proposed new towns at Evry and Tigery-Lieusaint.

Table 4 indicates that the eight proposed new towns were expected to accommodate approximately 4·5 million inhabitants by the end of the century.

Urban redevelopment and transport proposals
The *Schéma* foreshadowed major innovations in the agglomeration taking place along the two preferential axes described above, but more restricted development was envisaged in the suburban zone to the west and south of Paris. To the west work is already well advanced on the Défense redevelopment scheme, a suburban node established in the P.A.D.O.G. proposals and retained in the *Schéma Directeur*. This scheme involves office, cultural, and administrative developments and the complex is already linked by express Métro to central Paris. In addition La Défense is adjacent to the new university and *préfecture* of Nanterre, forming a rapidly-growing concentration of tertiary employment in the otherwise predominantly manufacturing area of the western inner suburbs. To the south of central Paris a major area of development was envisaged based on the activities of Orly airport and the new food market at Rungis. This too has already become a reality benefiting particularly from the motorway communications. Major industrial expansion was foreseen at Bonneuil and a large urban redevelopment scheme at Créteil the new *préfecture* of the Val-de-Marne *département*.

For the new towns and suburban nodes to function efficiently and for the unity of the agglomeration to be preserved within its enlarged dimensions, radical improvements in transport are clearly necessary. Accordingly, ambitious proposals were made in the *Schéma*, especially in

Photo 7. The *Réseau Express Régional,* the new station at Étoile

the sphere of mass transit systems. The major innovation foreshadowed was the extension of the *Réseau Express Régional* (R.E.R.), a combination of Métro and suburban railway with double the operational speed and line capacity of the existing Métro. The trains would run underground in central Paris, but elsewhere would be surface systems, in most instances using existing rail lines. The proposed network is illustrated in Fig. 7 consisting of a major east–west line, crossed by two north–south lines. The projected network was 260 kilometres long and would join the airports of Paris–Nord and Orly and, with the exception of Mantes–South, would connect all the new towns and most of the new suburban nodes with each other and with central Paris. Improvements to the road system included 800 kilometres of motorway and urban expressway. Two ring motorways, at between 10 and 15 kilometres from the city centre (the *Rocade de Banlieue*), and at 20 kilometres (the *Autoroute Interurbaine de Seine-et-Oise*), along with the *Boulevard Périphérique,* would be intersected by the motorways radiating from Paris, providing a comprehensive suburban and by-pass network.

The new town and transport proposals described thus far concern only the agglomeration and its immediate extension, which accounts for only 20 per cent of the Paris Region. A further 20 per cent of the region consists of woodland and the remaining 60 per cent of agricultural land with a scattering of small and medium-sized towns currently expanding at a high rate. The *Schéma* outlined a number of principles rather than specific proposals for this outlying zone of the Paris Région. A high proportion was zoned as amenity land, but it was estimated that the urban popula-

tion would double by the end of the century, the Oise valley in particular having a potential for rapid growth.

In summary, the *Schéma Directeur* forecast that by the year 2000 the central agglomeration would have a reduced population of 2·5 million, that the existing suburbs could increase from 4·7 to 7 million and that the new towns would double the size of the agglomeration and could house up to 4·5 million inhabitants. The remainder of the Paris Region would double its population giving a grand total at the end of the century of over 14 million inhabitants.

Revisions and realizations

The publication of the *Schéma Directeur* in 1965 marked a critical watershed in the evolution of Paris. No longer was disorganized development to be tolerated but instead planning more comprehensive in character and longer in time-span than anything previously envisaged was to be invoked. In view of this it is not surprising that the original proposals should be amended within a relatively short time. Continuing research, consultation with the Paris Transport Authority, the findings of the 1968 Census of Population, and above all the change of scale from regional structure plan to the preparation of detailed local plans, have all necessitated a reappraisal of the strategy and contributed important amendments. The overall axial strategy remains intact as does the principle of new town construction, but their number has been reduced from eight to five. Construction of a new town south of Mantes has been deferred in view of the decision to build a new town at Le Vaudreuil in the Seine Valley near Rouen. The carrying out of a major expansion project at Mantes could have compromised this and other urban expansion schemes in the Lower Seine Valley. Similarly, a new town at Beauchamp on the scale initially envisaged has also been deferred so as not to bring about massive and dense urbanization between the existing agglomeration and the new town at Cergy-Pontoise. On the southern axis the number of new urban centres at Trappes has been reduced from two to one so as not to prejudice the intended growth of Versailles as a strong suburban node, and also to restrain the south-western expansion of the agglomeration. The name St. Quentin-en-Yvelines is now applied to the single new town near Trappes.

The remaining new centres have been confirmed in the revised *Schéma*. The site of Tigery-Lieusaint has been redefined to a position closer to Melun in order to bring about an integrated development, and the name Melun-Senart has been adopted. The proposed new development in the Marne valley has been confirmed and the southern bank designated for a major new centre, Marne-La-Vallée, which will also function as a service centre for the eastern suburbs of Paris, counterbalancing the present trend for activity to gravitate westwards in the agglomeration.

The policy of strengthening nodal centres within the agglomeration is retained, with some modifications. The importance of Créteil is to be enhanced and additional urban centres have been designated at Vélizy-Villacoublay and at Le Bourget, the latter occupying the site of the airport scheduled for closure when Paris-Nord becomes operational. Modifications to the transport proposals include realignments of the *Réseau Express Régional* to take advantage of existing railway systems and several extensions of the Métro system into the suburbs. These revisions of the *Schéma* are summarized in Fig. 8.

The achievements thus far are at once both modest and impressive; modest in relation to the scale of the eventual development but impressive in the speed with which the strategic decisions have been translated into actual construction. In the case of the new towns, development corporations have been constituted for the five locations, detailed physical plans have been prepared, a start has been made on land acquisition, and the first stages of construction engaged. The suburban node of La Défense is now an impressive feature in the skyline of western Paris and the vast food market in the future Rungis node is operational. In the case of the *Réseau Express Régional*,

Fig. 8. Modifications of the *Schéma Directeur*

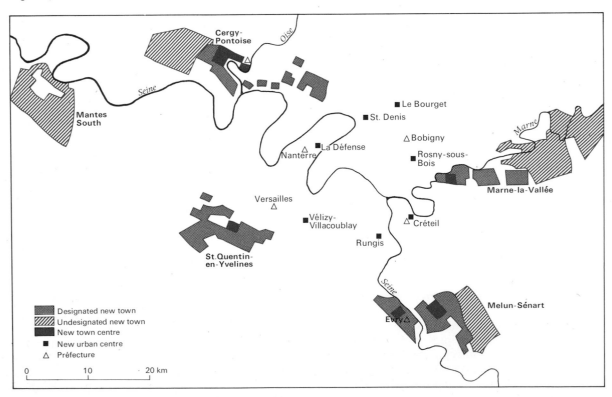

34

I.A.U.R.P.

Photo 8. Planning achievements: the Rungis food market complex

I.A.U.R.P.

Photo 9. Planning achievements: the *Réseau Express Régional* at La Défense, combined with a commercial centre

a major section of the east-west line is already in service. Important sections of intra-urban motorway, including a second motorway to Orly airport, have been completed, and the *Boulevard Périphérique* is approaching completion. The new airport of Paris-Nord is in an advanced stage of construction and is scheduled to handle its first flights in 1974. The decision has been taken in principle to construct a hovertrain link between Orly and Cergy-Pontoise. Further transport developments incorporated in the span of the Sixth Plan (1971–5) are illustrated in Fig. 9.

Physical planning in central Paris

The city of Paris was not included in the strategic proposals of the *Schéma Directeur* since this is the subject of a separate development plan. The *Schéma* nevertheless observed that the creation of

Fig. 9. Priority transport developments in the Paris region, 1971–5

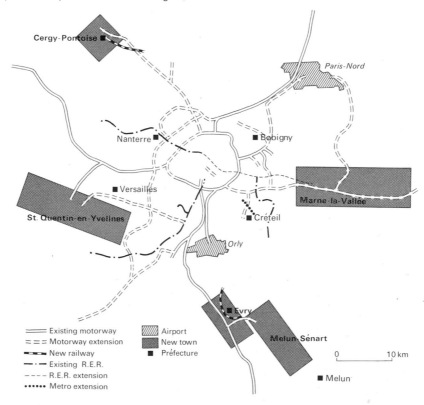

Cergy-Pontoise

Paris-Nord

Nanterre

Bobigny

Versailles

Marne-la-Vallée

St. Quentin-en-Yvelines

Créteil

Orly

Evry

Melun-Sénart

Melun

——— Existing motorway
=== Motorway extension
▬●▬ New railway
—·— Existing R.E.R.
----- R.E.R. extension
••••• Metro extension

▨ Airport
▩ New town
■ Préfecture

0   10 km

I.A.U.R.P.

Photo 10. The modern slab structures of the Maine-Montparnasse scheme of urban redevelopment. They have aroused controversy because of their proximity to the old buildings of the Left Bank with which they appear out of sympathy

new towns should not be allowed to compromise the political and commercial status of Paris on which its European and world role depends. Physical planning within Paris is thus concerned with enhancing the quality of the city from the point of view of residence, employment, and circulation.

The problem of renewing areas of decayed buildings and congested streets is being approached at two levels. A policy of renovation is being applied to a large number of areas, particularly in the eastern Marais and Belleville districts, involving the remodelling and modernization of groups of sub-standard buildings. Secondly, a more limited number of sectors are being redeveloped on a comprehensive scale involving major changes of function. The case may be cited of the Maine-Montparnasse redevelopment, commenced in 1961 on the site of the Montparnasse railway station. This scheme, now nearing completion has involved the construction of a modern railway terminus, adjacent office blocks, parking space, housing and street widening. Similarly, the Fronts-de-Seine occupies the site of a car factory decentralized from Paris, and includes new residential tower blocks and offices. Similar comprehensive redevelopments are planned for the site of the Halles food market, which will be served by the *Réseau Express Régional,* and for the waterfront at Bercy, near the Gare de Lyon. This latter scheme is seen as crucial in that it is envisaged as a counterweight to La Défense, and thus a means of checking the drift of activity westwards.

Transport planning within the city aims at im-

proving mass transit systems and easing the congestion of private vehicles. A key element will be the completion of the *Boulevard Périphérique* together with the likely construction of a Left Bank Expressway parallel to that already in existence on the right bank. Paris will then be equipped with radial approach motorways, an inner circular motorway, and two expressways bisecting the city. The congestion of the distributory roads within the centre can only be eased by a more rational system of parking. Multi-storey and underground car parks have been built at the motorway and trunk road entrances to the city in an attempt to divert car travellers to the public transport systems. Traffic meters have also been introduced in the city centre. Improvements in public transport include the introduction of larger buses using priority lanes and the interchangeability of bus and Métro tickets. The extension of the *Réseau Express Régional* should also divert commuters away from car travel to public transport.

As compared with the bold plans for new towns outside Paris, the proposals within the city are more piecemeal and diffuse. This reflects a number of constraints which limit the scale, character, and pace of development. Foremost of these constraints is the factor of cost. The acquisition of land, whether for new roads, offices, housing development, parking lots, or even simply for badly-needed additional open spaces, involves enormous cost in competition with other high priority calls on municipal and government funds. Further constraints are of a legal nature. The acquisition of land for motorways, which allow the minimum of flexibility in their alignment and involve the appropriation of land from a multitude of owners, implies prolonged legal proceedings which slow the pace of construction. Political constraints are also apparent in that major developments require complete co-ordination between numerous government departments and the municipal authority. The establishment of integrated decision-making and financing between several government departments and an authority representing a wide range of political parties can result in delays and postponements of critical projects. As a consistent backcloth to all these constraints is the need to preserve the aesthetic character of Paris. This involves not only the historic buildings, but also their immediate surroundings and even the larger prospect and vista of the major edifices.

Many instances have been cited of the practical effects of these constraints. The relatively slow pace of construction of the *Boulevard Périphéri-*

Photo 11. The *Boulevard Périphérique* near the Porte de Clignancourt

que, the soaring costs of the new meat market at La Villette, the postponement of major housing and commercial developments in eastern Paris, and the failure to complete many schemes on schedule reflect problems of finance, legal complications and political divergences. However, it is the question of maintaining aesthetic qualities that has aroused most public concern. This has focussed on three main issues which in the minds of the most severe critics add up to a rape of central Paris. A major concern is the destruction of entire *quartiers*, which although often in a state of physical decay and contributing to congestion, hold a great sentimental or aesthetic value both for Parisians and all who cherish traditional Paris. A specific case has recently highlighted this dilemma: the redevelopment of the Halles food market consequent on the decentralization of the meat market to La Villette and vegetable and fruit wholesaling to Rungis. The scheme involves the destruction of the market buildings, held by the conservationists to be of unique architectural interest, and the redevelopment of the surrounding area, which although sadly dilapidated, is one of the most distinctive *quartiers* of Paris and has a particular place in the city's folklore. In spite of fierce public outcry, the redevelopment is going ahead, the market pavilions making way for a new express Métro station, commercial, residential and cultural buildings; but it has been conceded that part of the market should be conserved for re-erection on a suitable site elsewhere.

A second concern is that virtually all new development is being planned in tower blocks of great height, consequent on the high land-values. Justi-fiable fear is being expressed that such skyscraper development is entirely out of harmony with the heritage of fine buildings in central Paris, most of which, with the obvious exception of the Eiffel Tower, are of modest elevation. Already the skyline of Paris has been transformed at La Défense and the Fronts-de-Seine, but these constructions are sufficiently distant from central Paris and are located in areas undistinguished by historical buildings. Moreover, they are in themselves examples of outstanding architecture and imaginative planning. Much more criticism has been levelled at the Maine-Montparnasse redevelopment, both because of its location in the Latin Quarter and in close proximity to the city centre, and because of the design of the buildings. Already, massive high-rise buildings have been completed (Photo 10) and a giant skyscraper, almost on the scale of the Eiffel Tower, will soon surmount the complex. Such architecture is clearly out of context with its location and the repetition of such schemes would destroy the harmony of the urban landscape of central Paris, mercifully preserved up until this time.

A third source of anxiety is the inexorable growth of road traffic and the resultant disfiguration as fine boulevards become in effect expressways, as new motorways are built through the heart of the city, and as the problem of noise and atmospheric pollution increases. This issue has become particularly controversial with the proposal to build a left bank expressway traversing the historic core of the city. The proposal has predictably raised widespread protest and the current discussions between the government and

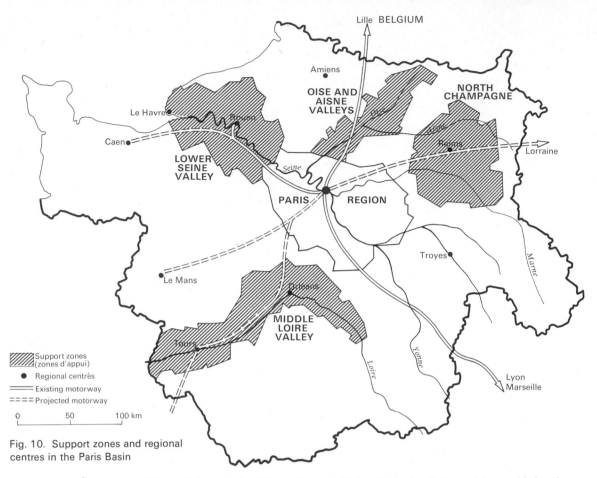

Fig. 10. Support zones and regional
centres in the Paris Basin

Map labels:

Lille BELGIUM

Amiens

Le Havre
Rouen
Caen

OISE AND
AISNE
VALLEYS

NORTH
CHAMPAGNE

Reims

Lorraine

LOWER
SEINE
VALLEY

Seine

PARIS   REGION

Le Mans

Orléans

Troyes

Marne

MIDDLE
LOIRE
VALLEY

Tours

Loire   Yonne

Lyon
Marseille

Legend:

Support zones
(zones d'appui)
● Regional centrès
Existing motorway
==== Projected motorway

0   50   100 km

Photo 12. Part of the port of Rouen. Islands in the Seine such as the Ile Lacroix in the photograph have added to the amount
of mooring available for barges

E. Kay

the municipal authorities are focussed on the environmental implications.

From this brief summary of planning constraints in central Paris it is evident that while the creation of new towns and suburban nodes outside the agglomeration offers a challenge to imaginative long-term planning, it is the restructuring and redevelopment of the heart of the agglomeration which poses the greater technical, political, financial, and conservation difficulty, and the problems demand immediate rather than long-term action.

Strategy for the Paris Basin

Two facets of recent planning in the Paris Basin have been described: the attempt to decentralize activity from Paris and the long term restructuring of the agglomeration. The third element of recent planning policy is the attempt that is now being made to plan for a more balanced development within the Paris Basin as a whole.

Earlier chapters have described the paradox of the juxtaposition of a world city, whose growth in recent decades has been too rapid, with a surrounding tributary region, the Paris Basin, in which urban and economic development has been modest until quite recently. Since the Second World War, some changes in this contrasted pattern have occurred. The restrictions placed on new industrial and office growth in central Paris have benefited the Paris Basin, even though comparatively little in the way of government financial inducement was involved. A spontaneous spilling-out of industry has occurred benefiting particularly the small towns within the immediate orbit of Paris and the towns of the Lower Seine Valley, but also reaching some of the more distant centres in the Paris Basin. This economic stimulus has been accompanied by demographic revival and especially an impetus towards urban expansion. The significance of routeways has been enhanced by the construction of motorways across the Basin to the north, south and west of Paris, and the electrification of all the main lines radiating from Paris. Major port investment, with the advent of super tankers, bulk carriers, and container vessels, has transformed the potential of the Le Havre area. New universities have been created at Rouen, Reims, Le Mans, Amiens, Orléans, Tours and Saint-Quentin. Finally, the influence of Paris has spread ever wider with the proliferation of second homes along the Normandy coast and in the wooded valleys of the Seine basin.

By the time the *Schéma Directeur* was published

some reversal of the trends of past centuries could be discerned. No longer was the Paris Basin being drained of population and activity, but on the contrary new growth was spreading outwards from Paris and several of the towns were expanding more rapidly than Paris itself. Nevertheless new planning problems had arisen partly because of this growth. The decision to build new towns adjacent to Paris, some of them larger than any existing towns in the Paris Basin, was seen as a threat to the continued urban expansion of established centres. The very rapid growth of the inner circle of towns as compared with the slower growth of those on the periphery of the Basin, particularly to the east and south, pointed to the risk of new distortion taking place. The threat to the environment as a result of urban growth and pollution of the main river valleys, was also cause for concern. Above all, the lack of detailed coordination between the plans for the Paris Region and those of adjacent planning regions, emphasized the need for an integrated strategy for the Paris Basin in its entirety.

Recognition of these problems resulted in the setting up in 1966 of an inter-ministerial group concerned with long-term planning in the Paris Basin. This group published its first report in 1968, which embodied several major decisions, the most important of which was the designation of four 'support zones' (*zones d'appui*), to be characterized by a high level of urbanization, increased powers of internal planning and administration, and suitable conditions to help in the decongestion of Paris by the reception of decentralized activities. The four areas designated were the Lower Seine Valley, the Loire Valley between Orléans and Tours, the valleys of the Oise and Aisne, and a sector of Champagne based on Reims (Fig. 10). Secondly, the nine regional centres of the Basin with over 100 000 inhabitants were to be strengthened with a view to extending their spheres of influence. For each of the *zones d'appui*, a structure plan was to be prepared similar in function to that of the *Schéma Directeur*. This 1968 report was followed by further discussion papers, and in 1970 a development plan integrating proposals throughout the Paris Basin was published as a policy basis for regional planning during the Sixth National Plan. This essentially followed the same strategy of directing towards the *zones d'appui* activities which need to be located close to Paris but which otherwise would add to the congestion of the agglomeration. Of the strategic plans, that of the Lower Seine Valley is the most advanced and most crucial and is thus worthy of some elaboration.

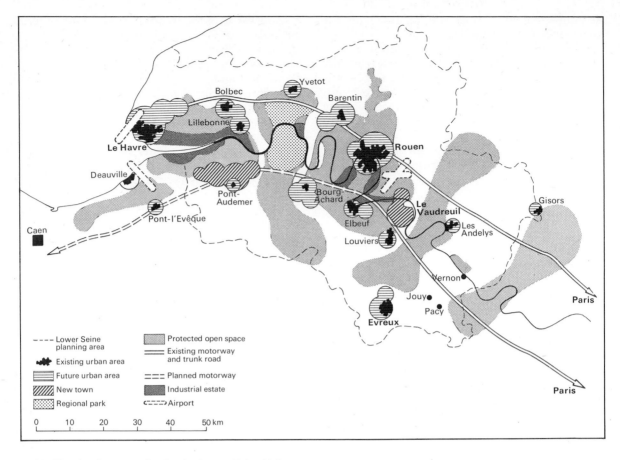

Fig. 11. The development plan for the Lower Seine Valley

The Lower Seine Valley Development Plan

The Lower Seine Valley is a strategic corridor linking Paris with Rouen, a major regional centre and inland port, and with Le Havre, the second maritime port of France. The valley thus has a long history of industrial and urban development but has always existed in the shadow of Paris. It is a strong line of movement followed by motorway, electrified rail, inland navigation, and oil and gas pipelines, and is a natural westward prolongation of the preferential axes of the *Schéma Directeur*. The planned port and industrial extensions at Le Havre, the chain of six petroleum refineries,

the acquisition of decentralized industries from Paris which is already quite pronounced, and the proximity to Paris all point to a high potential for further growth. The principal planning tasks are therefore to create an appropriate structure to accommodate growth (with a particular need to prevent ribbon development extending as a continuous tentacle from Paris), to protect land of high amenity value, and to resist the valley becoming simply a satellite of Paris.

The development plan was approved at the end of 1969 and is summarized in Fig. 11. The plan divides the area into three zones, the estuary,

TABLE 5
Projected population growth in the Lower Seine Valley

	1968	Present trend projected to 2000	Planned total in 2000
Estuary	400 000	800 000	895 000
Greater Rouen	860 000	1 100 000	1 180 000
Upstream from Rouen	315 000	600 000	425 000

Photo 13. The rebuilt town centre and port at Le Havre; in the background is the alluvial plain, site of the new industrial development

Greater Rouen, and the valley upstream from Rouen, with a present total population of almost 1·6 million inhabitants. The projected population growth based on present trends and the modifications to be achieved under the development plan are shown in Table 5.

It is clear from Table 5 that the plan calls for a slackening in the pace of urbanization between Rouen and Paris in accordance with the desire to prevent continuous urban sprawl along the valley from Paris. Fig. 11, summarizing the main proposals, indicates that this is to be achieved by the preservation of wedges of open land at intervals across the corridor. On the other hand, a somewhat accelerated growth is planned for Greater Rouen, consonant with the policy of strengthening the position of the regional centres of the Paris Basin. Much of this growth will be on the left bank, counterbalancing the present right bank concentration. A new town is to be built at Le Vaudreuil, 20 kilometres from Rouen, taking advantage of excellent motorway and rail communications and also of an outstanding waterside

and woodland setting. This new town is already scheduled for construction and will afford an ideal site for decentralized industry since it will not contribute to ribbon development too close to Paris and will enjoy proximity to Rouen without congesting that city.

The high growth target for the estuary zone is related to ambitious plans, already being fulfilled, to create a major port-cum-industrial complex at the mouth of the Seine. Le Havre is the only French Atlantic port able to accept giant tankers of 250 000 tons, and the newly opened maritime lock, the largest in the world, will permit tankers and bulk carriers to penetrate beyond the existing port into the heart of a vast new industrial estate being built on reclaimed land. The combination of deep water access and a wealth of unused industrial land give Le Havre the possibility of becoming a major European industrial complex by the close of the century. There are even plans for a giant offshore terminal to the north of Le Havre capable of receiving the largest tankers at present conceivable. The latter would not be able to

E. Kay

Photo 14. The Seine valley as an amenity: Les Andelys

negotiate the Straits of Dover. A proposed bridge at the mouth of the Seine would permit parallel development of the left bank—particularly important as residential development on the north bank is restricted by problems of atmospheric pollution from the existing refinery complex.

In addition to this port expansion, road transport is to be improved by extensions to the trunk road and motorway system. The problem of environmental conservation is to be met throughout the planning area by the preservation of belts of woodland and the provision of numerous waterside recreational areas. One forest tract, the Forest of Brotonne, has already been designated as a regional park.

The Development Plan for the Lower Seine Valley thus attempts to create a favourable structure within the area through rational policies of industrial location, urban expansion, and environmental protection, while at the same time being in harmony with policies for the Paris Basin

as a whole. For example, it is now envisaged that the unit should be extended to include the resorts of southern Normandy and the agglomeration of Caen, since these will inevitably become functionally absorbed into the economic and urban structure of the Lower Seine.

Other plans

The Development Plans for the other *zones d'appui* are less far advanced, but the planning issues involved are becoming clear. The designation of the Oise-Aisne zone is a consequence of its location between the two most powerful economic regions of France, the Paris agglomeration and the Nord industrial region. Although to a lesser extent than the Lower Seine, the area has for long had an arterial character, with canal and rail routes in particular being used for the transfer of coal and heavy industrial goods from the Nord region to Paris. The arterial character of the Oise-Aisne valleys has been reinforced by the

Photo 15. The loss of amenity in the Seine valley: industrialization near Rouen

E. Kay

completion of the Canal du Nord, the electrification of the Paris–Lille railway, and the construction of the Nord motorway. In addition, the area is traversed by major international connections from Paris to London, Amsterdam and Brussels. Its location close to the new Paris–Nord airport will also enhance the potential for growth. The combination of improved communications and the closeness of Paris has meant that many of the small and medium-sized towns, such as Creil, Compiègne, Soissons, Beauvais, and Saint-Quentin, until recently experiencing relatively slow growth, have now entered a phase of rapid expansion. Creil and Beauvais in particular have experienced the highest population growth rates of all the towns in the *couronne* of the Paris Basin. This stems from their suitability as spontaneous overspill centres for industry decentralized from Paris and for new industrial development in general. The main concern of the structure plan for the Oise-Aisne *zone d'appui* must therefore be

to promote a rational distribution of industry controlled through the creation of new estates, accompanied by continued improvements in transport facilities as the demand increases and by a rigorous protection of the environment in the face of urban encroachment. A further strategic matter is the likelihood that the lower Oise valley between Pontoise and Compiègne could emerge as a further axis of development tangential to the Paris agglomeration, ultimately complementing the preferential axes already described in the *Schéma Directeur*. Inevitably, therefore, the future growth of the Oise-Aisne *zone d'appui* must be closely co-ordinated with the strategic decisions taken in the context of the Paris Region plan.

The *zone d'appui* of the Middle Loire displays marked contrasts with that of the Oise-Aisne in its basic geographical character. The arterial form is less emphatic, for although the valley is followed by main road and rail routes the intensity of traffic is less, there is as yet no motorway, and the Loire is insignificant for inland navigation. Secondly the basis of urbanization is different, consisting of two large, and to some extent, rival agglomerations, Orléans (167 500 inhabitants) and Tours (201 600 inhabitants), with a much smaller centre, Blois, approximately equidistant between them. Both Orléans and Tours have experienced much new industrial growth and rapid population increase during the last decade. The excellent rail communications, which bring Orléans within one hour of the Capital, define the Middle Loire as potentially an ideal reception zone for activities decentralized from Paris. The area is sufficiently distant from Paris to avoid becoming embroiled in the planning difficulties of the agglomeration while at the same time remaining accessible from Paris. Planning problems therefore centre on the achievement of a sound internal structure for development, avoiding excessive congestion of the two principal towns but at the same time avoiding equally undesirable unplanned ribbon development between them. The preliminary structure plan envisages an integrated urban corridor, linked by motorway, but with protected rural wedges interposed across the valley. Regularization of the Loire channel, at present prone to inundations, will release land for building and for waterside recreation, permitting an overall garden city structure to be envisaged.

Plans for the Reims–North Champagne *zone d'appui* have not yet been completed, but a strengthening of the size and influence of Reims as a regional centre is indicated, and the construction of the eastern motorway from Paris to Lorraine will clearly be a factor of great importance in the design of the structure plan.

Outside the *zones d'appui*, future planned development while being guided by the overall policies laid down for the Paris Basin will be enacted within the existing regional planning framework. The area involved falls within the planning regions of Picardie, Champagne, Bourgogne, Centre, Haute-Normandie and Basse-Normandie (see Fig. 2). Development problems are most severe towards the fringe of the Paris Basin, particularly in the west and south marking the transition to less developed regions of France, and to the northeast where the Ardennes industrial region is experiencing a decline in its metallurgical industrial base. In these areas, the application of the general government policy of aid to industry offers the best prospect for development (see Fig. 5).

Conclusion

The problems of the Paris Basin owe much of their severity to the absence or ineffectiveness of planning in the past, resulting in the growth of Paris to the detriment of other centres in the Basin and permitting uncontrolled expansion within the agglomeration. An elaborate planning machinery now exists to direct the future development of Paris and to co-ordinate growth throughout the Paris Basin. It would be misleading to conclude from this that solutions have been found to all the problems discussed. On the contrary, the drawing up of complex plans, projected a quarter of a century into the future, in turn creates new problems and ambiguities. The example may be cited of the decision to establish new towns in an attempt to halt the centripetal forces exerted by Paris. These must be made viable in spite of their proximity to Paris and the strong attraction of employment in the city. On the other hand, the generation of economic and commercial activity in the new towns and suburban nodes must be achieved without compromising the quality and range of functions in central Paris on which its European and world eminence depends.

The existence of such ambiguities implies the need for flexibility in planning. As economic, demographic, social, and technological factors change, so the plans must be adapted to the new circumstances. That the P.A.D.O.G. proposals should be superseded by the *Schéma Directeur*, in turn subject to numerous revisions, is evidence of this process at work. It is erroneous, therefore, to think in terms of final solutions, but rather of a continuing process of planning within an overall strategy, the assumptions of which must be periodically reviewed.

Further Work

1 Further Reading

A valuable reference for this and several other volumes in the Series is P. Hall, *The World Cities*, 1966 (revised edition to be published 1972). I. Thompson, *Modern France: A Social and Economic Geography*, 1970, includes chapters on the Paris Region, the regional planning structure, Paris and the Provinces, and on industrial decentralization. The same topics are discussed in H. Clout, *The Geography of Post-War France*, 1972.

An historical survey of physical planning in Paris is A. Sutcliffe, *The Autumn of Central Paris—the Defeat of Town Planning, 1850–1970*, 1970. An outline of the *Schéma Directeur* is given in E. Sibert, 'Regional Plan for Greater Paris', *Town and Country Planning*, 1966, p. 23. Progress on its execution is described in J. Abraham, 'Changing Face of Paris', *Geographical Magazine*, 1968, No. 2, p. 129.

Other useful background works are G. Crone, 'The Site and Growth of Paris', *Geographical Journal*, 1941, p. 37; R. E. Dickinson, *The West European City*, 1951; J. Ardagh, *The New France*, 1970; M. L. Brayne, 'The New Paris Market', *Geography*, 1972, p. 47.

2 Map Study

Reference to detailed maps of the agglomeration is essential for effective use of this book. The most appropriate maps are Michelin, sheet 96, Environs de Paris 1 : 100000; and sheet 100, Sorties de Paris 1 : 50000. Appropriate topographic maps are Nouvelle Carte de la France au 100 000^e, sheets Paris, Versailles, and Melun. For the study of Paris in its broader setting the *Oxford Regional Economic Atlas of Western Europe*, 1971, is recommended.

3 Comparative Study

Compare the problems and planning strategies of London and the South-East with those of the

Fig. 12. The site of the new town of Le Vaudreuil

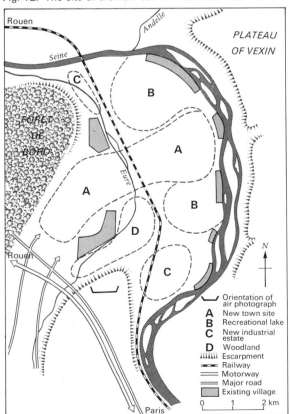

Photo 16. Aerial view of the site of Le Vaudreuil

Mission d'Etudes du Vandreuil

TABLE 6
Population change in the Paris Basin, 1962–8

Département	Population 1968	Rate of change 1962–8 %
Paris	2 581 796	−7·4
Seine-et-Marne	604 340	15·2
Yvelines	853 386	24·2
Essonne	674 157	40·6
Hauts-de-Seine	1 474 521	6·7
Seine-St.-Denis	1 251 792	15·5
Val-de-Marne	1 105 077	13·3
Val-d'Oise	693 269	26·4
Total Paris Region	9 238 338	9·0
Aisne	526 346	2·6
Ardennes	309 380	3·0
Aube	270 325	6·0
Calvados	519 695	8·1
Cher	304 601	3·8
Eure	383 375	5·9
Eure-et-Loire	302 207	8·9
Haute-Marne	214 336	2·8
Indre	247 178	−1·7
Indre-et-Loire	437 870	10·8
Loiret	430 629	10·5
Loir-et-Cher	267 896	6·8
Manche	451 939	1·1
Marne	485 388	9·8
Nièvre	247 702	5·0
Oise	540 988	12·4
Orne	288 524	2·8
Sarthe	461 839	4·2
Seine-Maritime	1 113 977	7·5
Somme	512 113	4·9
Yonne	283 432	5·0

Paris Basin. Reference should be made to *Strategic Plan for the South-East*, H.M.S.O., 1970, and to the commentary in P. Hall, *The World Cities*.

4 Aerial Photograph Analysis
Photo 16 is an oblique aerial view of the site of the new town of Le Vaudreuil, the main features of which are summarized in Fig. 12. Using this information and the location map, Fig. 11, consider the advantages and problems of the site and situation of this new town.

5 Industrial Decentralization
Suggest locations within the Paris Basin for the following two firms intending to decentralize from the Paris agglomeration: a precision engineering firm producing for world markets and intending to recruit 250 workers for its new factory; a vehicle assembly plant employing 1000 workers, the main component factories being retained in the

Paris agglomeration. Enumerate the criteria by which your choice is made and justify the selected locations.

6 Fieldwork
With the help of this text, further reading, and a suitable large-scale map, plan a five-day field excursion based on Paris designed to examine in the field the planning problems of the Paris agglomeration.

7 Map Exercise
Table 6 summarizes population data for the Paris Basin. Using this information, devise a series of maps (using proportional symbols, dots, or choropleths for example) to illustrate population distribution and change. In conjunction with Fig. 1 and Table 3, suggest possible explanations for the main contrasts in recent population changes in the Paris Basin.

Index